School Administrator's
September-June Almanac
of Events, Activities,
and Procedures

School Administrator's September-June Almanac of Events, Activities, and Procedures

Fred B. Chernow
Carol Chernow

Parker Publishing Company, Inc.
West Nyack, New York

©1977, *by*

PARKER PUBLISHING COMPANY, INC.

West Nyack, N.Y.

Library of Congress Cataloging in Publication Data

Chernow, Fred B
    School administrator's September-June almanac of
events, activities, and procedures.

    Includes index.
    1. Schedules, School--Handbooks, manuals, etc.
2. School management and organization--Handbooks,
manuals, etc. I. Chernow, Carol,   joint
author. II. Title.
LB1033.C47   371.2   77-8591
ISBN 0-13-792242-6

Printed in the United States of America

To daughters Barbara and Lynne—
shining examples
of our best administrative efforts.

How This Almanac Will Help You and Your School

This practical, comprehensive handbook provides tested programs organized in a way that will help you anticipate and simplify many of the problems encountered in school administration. The detailed guidelines, administrative techniques and programs describe specific ways to deal more effectively with such essential matters as teacher contracts, parental complaints, pupil unrest, and community pressures. The result will be a strengthened and more effectively planned and coordinated instructional program.

The "almanac" approach is of particular value because it will help you anticipate and prepare for every school situation. This extensive collection of practical administrative data is arranged conveniently into 11 monthly chapters, from September through June, plus one for summer activities. The arrangement is a flexible one, enabling you to select various activities out of sequence if you wish. Every key activity is included and can be quickly located. You will find the large number of sample forms particularly helpful because they are designed for easy adaptation to fit your particular needs. The hundreds of guidelines and tested ideas have been used successfully, and were drawn from the actual experience of frontline administrators in all parts of the country. They will help you improve and expand your skills as an administrator and

7

leader on any school level. For example, the book includes such features as...

- a "Planning Calendar" listing typical administrative duties during that month;
- an actual set of faculty conference notes for each month giving you ideas to spark your own faculty meetings.
- a selection of sample letters you can quickly adapt to meet your needs appropriate to that time of year;
- important matters that come up *throughout the year*, which will be brought to your attention in advance;
- specific guidelines for monthly activities that will actively involve parents and community leaders in a constructive way.

These ideas cover the full range of school administration, from the improvement of instruction to more efficient business management. The Almanac is organized for easy use, and the crystal clear, step-by-step directions, along with scores of examples, show you precisely how to use or adapt each suggestion most effectively.

By following the schedule in Chapter 10, for example, you will avoid those frantic days in June in which you try to balance pupil registers, hand out teacher ratings, and complete the many reports that are due prior to the close of school. Utilizing this chapter will demonstrate the dramatically effective results that can be yours. You and your staff will end the school year on a calm, efficient, confident note.

How often have you come up with a great idea for a school event only to realize that you can't get it off the ground because you don't have enough time? Chapter 3 will give you several school "celebration" ideas that you can plan weeks in advance. The valuable checklist will help you avoid last-minute pitfalls. Such basic and practical considerations as a simple assembly-use rehearsal schedule will help you avoid having two teachers trying to use the same room at the same time.

Chapter 8 will help to keep you from missing out on some special events that other schools carry off successfully, such as Ecology Day, Grade One Science Fair, a parent-planned International Luncheon, Olympics for the Handicapped, or a Nostalgia Night. Chapter 11 offers simple plans for the summer, that can save countless hours in getting off to a fast start in September. You'll be able to use a postcard that is mailed to each parent of an incoming student (in August), advising the pupil of his or her class, room, and line-up area. These cards are addressed and printed in June and merely dropped in the mail at the end of August.

A checklist of pre-opening day items will help you get the school year off to a smooth start in September. You will avoid the headaches of book and supply ordering when you follow the simple suggestions given in the March chapter. Dozens of invaluable, time-saving ideas not only include *when* you should put the plan into effect, but also describe how to take the action quickly and efficiently. For example, you will receive detailed guidance and how-to information on such things as:

- sample "Principal Messages" for yearbooks, parent newsletters, and graduation speeches;
- key items to plan for in teacher negotiations or grievances;
- easy-to-follow procedures for improving plan books or lesson plans;
- proven ways to insure a higher level of pupil and teacher school attendance;
- agenda of items for PTA meetings;
- arranging your daily time schedules more efficiently so you will be able to accomplish more—in less time.

Virtually nothing is left to chance. Compiled from successful programs developed by experienced, practicing administrators, this book will prepare you for the kinds of administrative problems you now face—or will in the future. You will want to turn frequently to this pragmatic, up-to-the-minute source book. The compendium of conference notes and principal's messages alone will save you many hours of work. You will be able to anticipate what needs to be done in connection with important events and due dates. You will be in control of the school calendar and not imprisoned by it. Inside the Almanac you'll find innovative thinking and step-by-step guidance that you can use in your own special situations. In short, you will pick up scores of proven and practical techniques that will insure your continued success as a school administrator—primarily because of the increased skill you'll acquire as a planner and a doer.

Fred B. Chernow and Carol Chernow

CONTENTS

Chapter 8—April (con't.)

Chapter 9—MAY ● 171

Chapter 10—JUNE ● 189

School Administrator's
September-June Almanac
of Events, Activities,
and Procedures

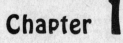

Chapter 1

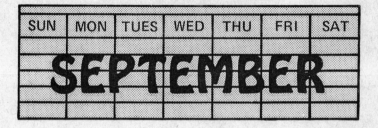

SUN	MON	TUES	WED	THU	FRI	SAT

SEPTEMBER

How to set up an orientation program

One of the most important functions of a school administrator at the beginning of the school year is to orient the staff. This includes welcoming back the "old" teachers as well as familiarizing the "new" teachers with the philosophy and practices of the school. This cannot be a slipshod or careless approach to staff members. To be effective, it must be carefully thought out and executed deliberately.

In some school districts there are several days set aside prior to the return of pupils for teachers to meet in their schools for purposes of orientation. In too many cases, this becomes a time for decorating the classroom and scrambling for books and supplies before the supply is exhausted.

Too often, the orientation is reserved for just the newly assigned teachers, and other staff members who could benefit from some direction are excluded. Through a well-planned orientation program the principal can help faculty members face problems that are experienced in the school and the community. A good program would include:

1. An introduction of all school personnel, including their special functions. In this way, health, clinical, remedial, supervisory, and administrative personnel would have a chance to explain their functions and roles to all the teachers.

2. A tour of the building, during which the locations of various services and offices are pointed out. Included would be the teachers' lounge and lunchroom, guidance office, medical room, etc.

3. Providing each teacher with an organization sheet that lists the name and class of every teacher as well as non-classroom personnel and their telephone extensions.

4. A conference with all new teachers to establish rapport, discuss school policy, and acquaint them with the socio-economic status of the community. Visit a community resource, such as the library or community center.

5. An individual meeting with each new teacher to discuss the composition of the class assigned, including a review of some of the pupil records. Discussion should include such essential items of class management as line-ups and dismissals, distribution and care of materials, and housekeeping chores.

6. Information on school routines involving milk and lunch programs, provision for sick children, ordering supplies.

7. Provision of helpful materials and schedules, such as instructions for emergency drills, curriculum bulletins, sample plan book, school handbook, "Some Tips to New Teachers" (see below).

8. Arrangement of the pairing of a new teacher and a "buddy" teacher who has already demonstrated success in the subject area or grade level.

All these activities should take place prior to the arrival of pupils. The following three items should take place on the first day of actual teaching in September:

1. Escort the new teacher to the classroom or yard line-up area and introduce him or her to the class. This will go a long way in helping the teachers get off to a good start with their classes.

2. Look in a few times to see if assistance is needed.

3. At the end of the first day, arrange a meeting to see if the teacher has any immediate problems or questions.

Effective tips for new teachers

You will want to give your teachers some necessary reminders as well as acquaint the new staff members with good school practices to follow. These tips fall into four basic categories and can be easily adapted to your particular school.

SOME TIPS TO NEW TEACHERS

School Organization

1. Become acquainted with the school's bell and gong schedules.
2. Learn the proper dismissal procedures for your class.
3. Be prompt in arriving and leaving out-of-room assignments.
4. Be sure you know your building assignments (play yard, lunchroom) and cover them conscientiously.
5. Check the school bulletin board each morning for official notices; clear out your letter box daily.
6. Hang your room keys on the proper hook in the office key cabinet before leaving the building. Do not entrust these keys to pupils.
7. Never leave money in school overnight. Be sure to keep your handbag in a secure place during the day.
8. Keep a school organization sheet available.

Safety

1. Learn immediately the proper procedures for fire and other drills for your room and other parts of the building your class may occupy.
2. Never leave a class unsupervised. If you must leave your room, notify the teacher in the nearest room and keep the doors of both rooms open.
3. Do not allow the pupils to stand outside your classroom unsupervised.
4. Have a health inspection as the day's first activity. Check to see if pupils appear alert and clean. Occasionally look at hair and scalp to see if they are free from lice.
5. Have girls in all grades and boys below Grade Four leave the room in pairs.
6. Never send pupils on errands outside the school building.
7. If a child is injured, administer first aid, if necessary, and notify a supervisor immediately.
8. Lock your door whenever you vacate your room and check to see that no child is left in the room.
9. Do not permit children to carry glass containers.
10. Use proper UP and DOWN staircases, except at general school arrivals and dismissals.

11. Have pupils carry out-of-room passes when leaving the room. Record their departure and arrival time in an Out-of-Room Book.

Discipline

1. Refer a disciplinary case to a supervisor on a referral card. (See Figure 1-1.) In an emergency, notify the office in writing.
2. Do not send the offender to the office unless notified to do so.
3. Never administer corporal punishment. It is forbidden by this Board of Education. (See note below, under "Handling punishment of pupils," where such punishment is permissible.)
4. Do not detain a child for disciplinary reasons at lunchtime or after school unless you have notified the home.
5. Do not punish the entire class for offenses committed by individual pupils.

Records

1. Do not take official records, such as roll books and record cards, from the building.
2. Keep your roll book in the proper desk drawer and your record cards in the metal container in the appropriate closet.
3. Have attendance sheets ready at the required time.
4. Record personally your time of arrival and departure each day. (This will vary from time clocks to entry books.)

SAMPLE REFERRAL CARD

Pupil's Name:_____Class: _____Room:____
Date of Incident:_____Reporting Teacher:_____
Description of Incident:_____
_____
_____
_____
Action taken by teacher:_____
_____
_____
Was parent notified? Yes_____No_____   How?____
Date card sent:_____ To whom?_____

FIGURE 1-1: Referral Card

Handling punishment of pupils

In 1975 the United States Supreme Court upheld the use of corporal punishment in schools provided that school staff members follow minimum due process procedures. In a summary judgment, upholding a lower court ruling without a hearing, the high court ruled in *Baker* vs. *Owen* that states may permit school teachers to spank misbehaving students—even over the objections of parents—as long as the teacher uses a lesser punishment when appropriate and warns the pupil ahead of time what kinds of behavior warrant a spanking. The ruling does not invalidate state laws that prohibit corporal punishment, such as in Massachusetts and New Jersey. It does not invalidate local laws established by boards of education. If your state or local authority bans the use of corporal punishment, this ruling of the court does not now make it permissible.

It does set up certain minimum standards which states must observe. The Supreme Court, by affirming the lower court opinion that corporal punishment is not "cruel and unusual punishment," ruled that corporal punishment is not unconstitutional. The ruling involved a sixth-grade pupil in North Carolina who was paddled for playing ball when he was not supposed to. The child's mother had asked that her child not be spanked because he was "frail" and said that such punishment violated her right to "familial privacy." But the lower court held that while the 14th Amendment to the Constitution includes the right of a parent to generally control the means of disciplining her child, "the state has a countervailing interest in the maintenance of order in the schools" and could administer "reasonable" corporal punishment. The court specifically said, however, that three criteria must be met: spanking should not be the "first line" of punishment; a second teacher must observe the punishment; and parents can get a written explanation of the punishment if they want one.

As one school administrator summed up the ruling: "It's nice to have a right you probably shouldn't use." It is important that you communicate to your teachers just what is your district and school policy in this important matter.

Referral Cards

The Discipline Referral Cards should be distinctive in color so that pupils will begin to know them as a "blue card" or a "pink card." This brief, descriptive nomenclature carries more weight among student folklore than the longer title. Once or twice a year, the administrator or dean of discipline should make two summaries—one by offense and a second by referring teachers. The results of such a survey will be well worth the time they take. At a glance you will be able to see what kinds of offenses are most annoying to teachers and get reported. Also, you will see which teachers send in the most referrals and which send in few or none. A third survey would tell you which times during the year seem to produce the most pupil unrest.

Out-of-Room Book

This should be any bound, lined notebook, preferably hung by a string somewhere near the classroom door. Pupils who can write their names unassisted record in the book their name, time left, destination, and time returned. Younger children would need to have this information recorded for them. Such a book serves many purposes. If there is some untoward incident in the hallway or bathroom, a quick inspection will show which pupils were out of their room at that time. If certain pupils seem to leave the room very often, the teacher has a written record to share with the parent during conference time. For some children this book serves as a deterrent against leaving the room when it is not necessary.

The room pass can be a rectangle of heavy cardboard or wood with the room number on it. When he is carrying the pass the child can easily be identified as coming from a particular room. The affording to each room of just one pass puts a natural limitation on the numbers of pupils out of the room at one time. Where there are several floors or wings to a building, pupils are discouraged from wandering to unauthorized areas by the easily read room number on their passes. In addition, a permanent room pass does away with the need for the teacher to stop and write out an individual excuse for pupils out of his or her classroom.

Setting up schedules that work

A schedule is a tool of instruction and not something that imprisons instruction. In recent years, newer forms of scheduling, particularly modular scheduling, have aroused much interest. Many schools use a block schedule. In a block of time, the principal provides teachers and students with options. A rotation schedule provides a simple, effective, and speedy variation in the school day. Merely rotating the order of class periods so that on one day the school begins with Period 2 and Period 1 is the last period of the day, on another day the school begins with Period 3 and Periods 1 and 2 are at the tail end of the day, and so on, will provide a change of pace for a staff.

These rotation schedules can be used to provide double periods, six or more days per cycle, or for other purposes needed in your school. The advantages of rotation schedules in the secondary school include ease of implementing and ease of determining whether the teachers can stand simple change.

A great deal of in-service training for teachers is necessary if these kinds of schedules are to be used most effectively. If you are concerned about your ability to initiate such a change, by all means avoid doing so until you know the schedule ramifications thoroughly. If you want to make a change in schedule, a simple rotation plan or a more challenging block schedule plan should precede any movement toward a modular schedule. Those who insist upon modular scheduling should solicit the assistance of experts in computerized scheduling.

In the elementary school the job of scheduling is far simpler. Most of the classes are self-contained. While there is some need to schedule classes into the library or gym or math lab, they are accustomed to spending most of their time in their homeroom. This does not mean that you should not have ready for the opening week of school a carefully drawn-up schedule of classes. In this way, each teacher will know his or her program and will consequently feel more secure.

Proper scheduling also helps you avoid problems such as two teachers trying to use the same area at the same time. Mrs. B.

brought her class down to the auditorium, intending to rehearse her fourth-grade class play. When she arrived she found the first grade on the stage going through a dry run of their Park Fete. If there had been an Auditorium Use schedule this confusion would not have taken place.

In those school districts where teachers get a free or unassigned preparation period, it is imperative that a clear schedule be produced for all the teachers and other personnel to refer to.

Besides daily schedules there are a host of weekly and monthly schedules that help smooth the flow of teacher assignments. For example, there might be a weekly duty roster of teachers scheduled for lunch duty or a monthly schedule of teachers and classes assigned the responsibility of putting up a hall bulletin board. Bus duty and hall patrol assignments are best listed on a duty roster that all can see and refer to.

Another helpful device that should be prepared in September is a roster of all members of the school staff and the location of their operations. This is sometimes called an "Organization Sheet" (see Figure 1-2). In addition to containing the names of the administrators, their office locations, the teachers and their class assignments, it should also list the telephone extensions for these people. In the case of a teacher or coordinator who is on a split assignment and visits the school only certain days of the week, this too should be noted on the organization sheet.

Notice how easy it is to see on which days the itinerant personnel are in the school and on which intercom extension they can be reached. Each class is designated with the grade followed by the room number. This is better than trying to show the track of each class by calling them 5-1 or 3-2. While it does not take long for the pupils to know which class on each grade is the top class, it works out better to designate all classes by grade and room.

These organization sheets can be enhanced even further by listing other vital information such as the fire drill signals or the bus schedules. Each principal will have to decide how detailed to make these sheets.

Planning for trips

It is not too early in the school year to help your teachers plan field trips. This is also the time to set up specific guidelines as to the

Public School 15   Francis Gould, Principal
School District 4   442-6123, Ext 2

ORGANIZATION—September 1976

5-317	Mrs. Powell	2-219	Miss Morris
5-319	Mrs. Roose	2-217	Mrs. Falco
4-303	Mr. Flynn	2-215	Ms. Cohen
4-305	Mr. McGowan	1-212	Ms. White
3-312	Miss Cook	1-214	Miss Bush
3-313	Mrs. Burke	1-215	Mrs. Markos

Guidance—Mr. Ellis, X-12
    (M, T, Th)

Library—Mrs. Holden, X-14

Custodian: Mr. Gantzen, X-20

Nurse: Mrs. Olsen, X-18

Speech: Miss Nunzio, X-16
    (M, W, F)

Drug Coordinator: Mr.
    Freeman (Wed. only)

Kgn 101   Mrs. Schneid
Kgn 105   Miss Armstrong
Kgn 109   Miss Gevins

Secretaries:
    Mrs. Dietz, X-10
    Miss Sakner (T, F)

Lunchroom: Mrs. Mon-
    tanti, X-17

Aides: Room 114, X-14

Mrs. Lee
Mrs. Betts
Mrs. Shaw
Mrs. Sanchez

FIGURE 1-2: Organization Sheet

types of trips and the kind of preparation and follow-up you expect. There are some teachers who never take classes on trips, while other teachers are quick to take trips but don't plan them carefully or capitalize on them back in the classroom. The majority of teachers do plan trips carefully and make use of them in the curriculum. All teachers, however, will benefit from this checklist:

1. Do you have fresh sources of ideas for trips? Pupils tire of going to the same place, year after year. Aside from those already known to you and your colleagues, several other ideas can be found in:

● The advertisements in magazines and newspapers.

- The yellow pages of your telephone directory, for museums, laboratories, factories, and art galleries.
- Locations recommended by local museums, professional groups, service organizations, and clubs.

2. Have you written to the specific site you are considering to determine:

- If they permit student tours on weekdays.
- What their hours are and if there is a fee.
- How many students they admit per tour.

3. If they indeed welcome pupils of your age group, you can now make preparations in earnest.

- Get school clearance and clear schedules.
- Obtain parent permission and chaperones.
- Charter a bus or arrange other transportation.
- Orient pupils and prepare them for what they will see.
- Plan follow-up activities.

4. Do your pupils know the answers to these questions:

- Why was this site selected?
- What will the cost of transportation be?
- Where do I get a consent form and when must it be in?
- Do I bring my own lunch; will there be a place to buy a drink?

5. Can your teachers answer these questions satisfactorily?

- Are any other school events scheduled for the same day?
- Have you discussed with the pupils their role as representatives of the school?
- Have you prepared a sheet of instructions on the specifics of the trip?
- Have you visited the facility to identify the highlights?
- Have you prepared a set of questions on the exhibits to draw pupil attention?
- Have you broken the group down into small groups for adult supervision?
- After the trip have you made notes on your own findings or difficulties encountered to help you on the next trip or to help other teachers going to this site?

At a faculty conference you can spark teacher interest by asking your staff to respond to these problem situations that may arise. You will be amazed at how well they can come up with cogent and convincing answers.

Problem #1. Some parents object to your taking your classes on so many field trips. Some of them have said that their children are in school to learn "basics." Your principal has asked you to explain to a meeting of parents the values of field trips. Describe in detail a class trip you are going to take or have taken. Document the values that this trip has for the students in your classes.

Problem #2. In your secondary school several of your colleagues object to your taking your class on a field trip because they are called upon to cover the remainder of your school program of classes and assignments. How would you answer their complaints?

Problem #3. In the spring, you have planned a day trip to an outdoor site such as a wildlife preserve. On the day of the trip there is heavy rain. The weather forecast is for more showers. What would you do? What would you say to pupils and/or parents?

Using these facsimiles or real problem situations is a good way to liven up a faculty conference. Every teacher feels he or she is an expert in at least one area of education. This forum gives the experienced teachers a chance to share their expertise with newer members of the staff. It gives the less experienced teachers a chance to hear from their colleagues and to get a full spectrum of advice and counsel on a given situation.

To help you not to miss out on any item of trip planning, we have prepared some sample forms that you may want to adapt for your school. (See Figures 1-3, 1-4, and 1-5.)

Attending to roll books

One of the more mundane responsibilities of teachers is the maintenance of a roll book where pupil attendance is checked. The format of the roll or attendance book varies in different school systems but the requirement for accuracy is the same everywhere. In many localities the amount of state aid is dependent on the percent of pupil attendance. This is still another reason why an accurate book must be kept. Whenever a pupil is injured in school and a court case ensues, the roll book is summoned to court to

John Adams School

Mary Godfrey, Principal

TRIPS

(To be filled in as soon as trip is definitely scheduled.)

Class	Date of trip	Destination	Transportation*	Applications to office**	Approved from District Office	Number of adult escorts. Separate P—Parents ST—Student Teacher	Consent slips on file***	Number of children going on trip.***	Names of children remaining in school. Room to which they are assigned for day.***

* Enter: Bus, Subway, Ferry, Walk.

** At least two weeks before date of trip.

*** To be filled ... just before class leaves the school for trip. No child may go unless there is a consent slip on file

FIGURE 1-3: Trips

ascertain how many days the child was absent from school. Other legal procedures involving custody of children require an inspection of the roll book by social and court agents. It is important that every teacher read the introductory pages in the roll book and adhere to the rules for entries. There is no substitute for periodic collections of teachers' roll books by the supervisor to see that they are being attended to properly. Emphasize that the roll book is a legal document. Encourage teachers to be neat and to make entries daily. If they wait until the end of the week they may not be recording the pupils' attendance accurately.

The sample checklists shown in Figures 1-5 and 1-6 will give you some ideas of what to look for.

Date _____

To the Principal of Public School_____

    I respectfully request that my son (daughter) of class_____
be permitted to take part in the extracurricular activity indicated by my initials below:

(   ) Excursion on_____ to_____.
(   ) Attend Field Day at athletic field.
(   ) Participate in games and athletic program at field.
(   ) Assist in monitorial duties as member of the Service Squad.
(   ) Serve on Safety Squad at street posts.
(   ) Class demonstration at_____.
(   ) Attend meeting of after-school_____ club.
(   ) _____
(   ) _____
(   ) _____
(   ) _____

                Very truly yours,

    Signature _____
                    Parent or Guardian

    Address _____
               _____

FIGURE 1-4: Consent

Joan of Arc School   Miss Agnes O'Dowd, Principal

TRIPS AND EXCURSIONS

1. Pupils and teachers should plan the trip together. Included in the planning should be:

    a. Purpose of the trip (what do we want to find out?).
    b. Details of transportation (time, costs, etc.).
    c. Briefing of pupils on their responsibilities as representatives of the school (including behavior and attire).
    d. Briefing of pupils on what they will see and do.
    e. Provision for evaluation and follow-up.

    Pupils must understand that the purpose of the trip is primarily educational and not recreational. They must understand that the learning experiences of the trip will be discussed and evaluated later and that the trip is part of their curriculum just as much as the textbook work or classroom discussion.

    Do not take trips to places that your pupils have already visited in lower grades.

2. *Procedures for Arranging Trips*

    Teachers planning to take a trip should first secure the approval of the principal. The District Office will *not* approve trips to movie theaters.

    After obtaining the necessary approval, the teacher will arrange for the trip with the agency or place to be visited. Following the confirmation of the date scheduled, the attached form must be filled out. Be accurate! List each class and the number of pupils.

    All pupils in the class should be taken!

    Arrangements must be completed and approval from District Office obtained at least five weeks before the trip. *DO NOT telephone the District Office—all arrangements will be made in writing.*

3. *A Few Do's and Don'ts*

    a. Do your best to adhere to your time schedule while on your trip. Call the school in case you are delayed or if a problem arises.

FIGURE 1-5: Trips and Excursions

b. Instruct pupils taking the trip not to arrive at school too early. Teachers conducting the trip must arrive at school early enough to supervise the arrival of pupils.

c. Speak to your supervisor before the trip to obtain information as to where the pupils may wait for the arrival of the chartered bus. Proper planning will prevent confusion.

d. Trips are made from the school; we are responsible for the pupils *until they return to school! DO NOT allow pupils to leave the bus in order that they may have a shorter trip home.*

e. Before leaving the school the teacher must have a consent slip for each pupil and a passenger manifest listing the pupils who actually went on the trip. *No pupil may accompany a teacher on a trip unless a parental consent slip is on file.*

f. Do obtain help of parents on your trip; one adult for each 15 pupils is mandatory in grades 3, 4, 5. In kindergarten—2, follow a 1/10 ratio.

g. Do not deviate from the planned itinerary for which you obtained permission from the District Office.

h. If you have any difficulty with the bus company, let your supervisor know.

FIGURE 1-5 (continued)

Class_____ Room_____ Teacher_____ Attendance Per.___

CHECKLIST FOR ROLL BOOK	1	2	3	4	5	6	7	8
Please read the introductory pages in your roll book and correct the following checked items:								
1. Roll book is a *legal document.* Erasures are not permitted. All corrections should be made in *red ink.*								
2. The inside front cover should have the statement, "I have checked the address of every child," as well as apartment number. Initial and date on monthly basis.								

FIGURE 1-6: Roll Book

Class Room Teacher Attendance Per.__							
CHECKLIST FOR ROLL BOOK	1	2	3	4	5	6	7	8

3. Use a *P* to indicate a postcard has been sent on first day of *unexplained* absence (bylaw of Bd. of Education). USE RED INK.

4. Use a T—absentee referral—form 407 is sent. (Should be sent on fifth day of consecutive unexplained absence and immediately in cases of known truants, known unlawful absence or suspiciously sporadic absences.)

5. Complete entries for period(s). Note: 1/2-day absences should not be combined and totaled as whole days; i.e., $1/2 + 1/2 = 2$ $1/2$'s and not one whole day.

6. Complete daily totals column each day. A pupil is to be counted present for the day if he has been under instruction for at least one hour on that day. NOTE: The completed sum of boys' "Daily Totals" added to the girls' "Daily Totals" should be the same as the total in column #6 on the attendance sheet.

7. In the admission or discharge column, note A or D and date effective. On discharges, draw a red ink line through the name and enter reason, address, etc. on Misc. Info. page.

8. Enter the proper data on the inside front cover when the whole class was excused for clerical half-days, parent reporting days, snowbound days, etc.

9. Initial each period_____

Supervisor:_____

TEACHER'S INITIALS

FIGURE 1-6 (continued)

P.S. 4   Brockport, Penna.
                                          December 8, 19___

MEMO: RE ROLL BOOKS

The Bureau of School Audit will be here within the next few days to check roll books.

Please be sure that your roll book is in good order. Read carefully pages 1 and 5 of the roll book and make especially sure that:

1. All entries are in blue or black ink.
2. All corrections are in red ink.
3. Latenesses are properly recorded.
4. Daily totals are entered at the bottom of the page.
5. Attendance period sub-totals and totals are entered. Check your arithmetic. Totals should equal the number of days in the marking period(s).

   (The sum of boys'
   (and girls' daily
   (totals should
   (equal the total
   (in Col. #6 on the
   (attendance sheet.

6. Released time is indicated thus ⊐▷R◁⊏ ; also, in pencil in front of pupil's name (R).
7. Admissions and discharges are properly recorded. Add data under "Miscellaneous Information."
8. The sending of postcards is noted with a red P. Clinic attendance is shown with a red C.
9. The sending of absentee referral forms (erroneously called "truant slips") is recorded with a red T.
10. Days on which the entire class was excused from attendance are noted on *the inside of the front cover.* To date they include:
    Dec. 2nd, Parent Teacher Conference Half-Day
11. An example of "notes" in the back of the roll book would be:
    "Jan. 13 Snowstorm."
12. Addresses and phone numbers are checked *periodically*. Complete all items on the front cover.

    The official place for the roll book is the top desk drawer.

Remember, your roll books are legal documents. In the past they have been used in trials of all kinds. Please get into good clerical habits, especially in marking the P.M. attendance.

FIGURE 1-7: Memo

Analysis of homeroom activities

If your school has "block" programming, that is, classes that move as a body from one subject area to another, then your homeroom teachers may meet their homeroom classes again in the course of the day. In schools with departmental organization, or modular scheduling, only some of the pupils who are in a given homeroom might also have their homeroom teacher as their subject teacher.

Whether or not your teachers meet their homeroom students again in one of their subject classes, it is important that you establish in September the kind of relationship that should exist between the homeroom teacher and his or her class. The tone of your school will in large measure depend on how successfully you do this.

From the standpoint of the administrator there are important duties that must be performed by the homeroom teacher:

Providing a channel of communication;
Accounting for pupils and keeping records;
Assisting in guidance activities;
Developing morale and school spirit.

In providing a channel of communication, it is in the homeroom rather than the subject classes that all school organizations, clubs, and extracurricular activities make contact with your students. Be sure to get the support of your teachers in keeping lines of communication open among the yearbook staff, honor society, teams, student council, placement counselor, and other vital school functions. If you do not establish the importance of the homeroom teacher in this regard in September, many students will be shut out by his or her indifference.

Point out the importance of accounting for pupils and keeping records. The homeroom record of attendance, lateness, and cutting is an essential guidance tool. The teacher's record of this information becomes a legal record for statistics that determines local, state, and federal financial aid. In the event of a student's claim of accident, or of truancy and violation of the attendance regulations, it constitutes the official school record. It is also useful for reports to parents or guardians.

Assisting in guidance activities is another important aspect of the role of homeroom teachers. They must know the location of the resource people to be contacted by the students. At the start of the school year you should conduct an orientation session for teachers new to the school. At this time, introduce your teachers to the school resource people, and instruct them in school procedures and regulations. For example, where are late passes issued? Who takes care of requests for medical appointments? How are working papers issued? The homeroom teacher is the students' first recourse in answering questions about programs, plans for the future, and difficulties in any of their subject classes.

Developing morale and school spirit is a major contribution of the well-trained homeroom teacher. Schools that have departmental or modular scheduling usually find that the homeroom is the best unit to work with for schoolwide activities. If, for example, the entire school were to go on a field trip—a Field Day—it is most likely that the school administration would organize the activity through the homerooms. Every student, despite the uniqueness of his or her program, has a homeroom. He or she "belongs" to some homeroom teacher who is accountable for him or her. Thus the homerooms are the arteries through which school spirit and morale are developed. The enthusiasm you generate among your homeroom teachers will filter down to the student body.

At a faculty conference you may want to throw out this general question for teachers to discuss: "You have three alternatives for seating students in your class: alphabetically, randomly, or letting them select their own seats. Discuss the advantages and limitations of each of these alternatives. Which would you use in a homeroom, which in a subject class?"

September straight talk

September is a good time to take a few quiet moments, most likely outside the school day, to reflect on your role as administrator in the year ahead. Your responsibility is mind-boggling in that students, parents, teachers, and the community all look to the principal for inspiration and direction. Yours is a key position requiring the energy and skills of a forthright, direct leader. Recent developments in the courts and in teacher contracts have made many principals too cautious to be effective leaders. The principal in today's schools must be aware of the legal restraints, of course, but he or she must also be aware of his or her rights to administer a school. A principal cannot hide behind the shortcomings of others.

No matter what the faults are of the school board members or the superintendent, the principal must be a strong leader in the school. His or her style is a matter of strategy and personality, but his or her strength in leadership must be obvious to the staff and to the community.

As principal you can hide behind the policies of the superintendent or school board, the demands of the teacher union, and the wishes of segments of the community, but in the building you are the boss. The word "principal" means "main" or "chief." You'd better be the chief or main something in your school or some other forces will fill the vacuum.

In too many schools the parent leader or union chairman has assumed too many prerogatives of the main or chief school person. This can only be done where the principal has abdicated the position.

This September make it your resolve that management details of a clerical nature will not prevent you from exercising organizational and instructional leadership. With simple delegation and/or avoidance of some clerical tasks, the principal can find some time each week to plan the school's direction. If you become effective in planning you may learn to like that aspect of leadership and then you will find more time for it. Once you realize this you will find the opportunities to demonstrate the courage of your convictions. The principal of today is often thought of as being pushed and shoved by various "groups" or elements. You will find that by assuming a posture of strength you will not be pegged as a pushover.

Sample conference notes

FACULTY CONFERENCE
September

A good teacher in the course of the day utters three times
as many compliments as critical statements.

—Baltimore Bulletin of Education

I. Personal.

    1.1   Welcome back of all personnel.

    1.2   Best wishes to Mrs. Ives upon her retirement.

1.3 Congratulations to Mrs. Collins, formerly Miss Lee.

1.4 Position changes:
Miss Smythe from Music to Grade 4.
Miss Forde from Grade 4 to Reading.

II. Administration.

2.1 School Safety Council—Mrs. Paine.
Description and aims.

2.2 Lunchroom—Mr. Gilmore.
Review rules:
Children who eat in school may not leave the building.
Bag lunch pupils are seated after the hot lunch pupils.

2.3 First day procedures:
Exchange records.
Check folders for change of register.
Compare class lists with roll books.
Notify book room of requests in writing.
Distribute schedules and programs.

2.3 Notice of September meetings:
Local school board—September 11.
Parents Advisory Council—September 19 at 7:30 P.M.

2.5 First Aid Kits: A first aid kit will be found in the following offices and rooms:
General Office
Principal's Office
Gymnasium
Vice-Principal's Office
School Aide's Room

III. Supervision.

3.1 Books:
Make sure that every child has a book in each subject area.
Check to see that textbooks are covered. Covers are available in aide's room.
Do not send all the books home every night.
List the prices of lost books on the chalk board.
Have each pupil sign a book card.
Check to see that pupils are not writing in their books.

3.2 Homework:
Be certain that children get some homework every night.

Check the homework each day for completeness and neatness.

Homework should be checked for accuracy.

Vary the kind of homework given each night.

3.3   Pupil written work:

Display samples of pupil written work on the bulletin board.

Correct all written work.

Keep folders on each pupil. Have him or her keep samples of written work in the folder.

Periodically send samples of written work to the office.

3.4   Classroom appearance:

Display many samples of pupil work. Art work as well as test papers should be on boards.

Train pupils to keep their floors clean.

Arrange to have pupils wash the boards daily.

Set up curriculum corners: science, art, listening center.

SEPTEMBER CURRICULUM CALENDAR

*Labor Day. Invite labor union officials to talk at pupil assemblies about significance of their contributions to the world of work.

10—American Indian Day. Have librarian prepare a display of books on native Americans. Encourage older pupils to look up names of local tribes.

15—Birthday of Grandma Moses. Use this as a springboard for a discussion in classrooms of the role of senior citizens and the increased availability of leisure time. Teachers can make use of this opportunity to study primitive art. Lower grade classes can use her paintings to study life in New England.

*Rosh Hashannah. Celebration of Jewish New Year. Have teachers point out the differences between present-day and lunar calendars. Pupils will understand why Jewish New Year and Christian Easter fall on different dates each year.

*Citizenship Day and Constitution Week. Use this opportunity to launch school student council. Emphasize the need for all citizens to be concerned with their community. Help pupils understand how a constitution protects them.

22—First Day of Autumn. Suggest that teachers use this opportunity to show how rotation of the earth and its revolving around the sun affects day and night and seasons of the year.

Better Breakfast Month. Use this opportunity to develop units on nutrition and health. Make a survey to see what your pupils eat for breakfast. Talk to parents at PTA meeting about the need for proper nutrition.

*National Hispanic Heritage Week. Highlight geographic closeness of Puerto Rico and Caribbean Islands. If appropriate, list the different island backgrounds of pupils in the school. Make a hall display of Hispanic flags.

*Exact date varies from year to year.

Chapter 2

SUN	MON	TUES	WED	THU	FRI	SAT
		OCTOBER				

Getting your buses rolling

A fact of life in the school business is that large numbers of pupils are transported to and from school by bus. It is the administrator's responsibility to apprise parents of bus stops and routes, schedules, safety, and deportment. October is a good time to reinforce the parents' responsibilities in these areas. By early October there should be some stability in the schedules and familiarity with the drivers and routes. It is not too early for youngsters to begin misbehaving on the bus, and it is your job to inform the parents of such pupil behavior.

As soon as practicable, send home a notice similar to the one shown in Figure 2-1 outlining the rules for bus pick-up and the stops the bus will make. Notice also that the parent signing this form is acknowledging his or her responsibility for informing pupils of the need for good behavior.

At least once each year a child will be reported again and again for misbehavior on the bus. After warning the child and the parent orally it may be necessary for you to send a letter home, withdrawing bus privileges for a short period of time. This will have a salutory effect on all the other children who ride the bus. You may want to modify the letter shown in Figure 2-2.

Pupils in kindergarten, first and second grade who live a half-mile or more from school are eligible to ride the school bus. Pupils in grades 3 through 6 who live more than one mile from school are also eligible.

Your child will board the bus at the stop nearest your home. He may begin as soon as you have signed this consent form. In an emergency when it is necessary for you to take your child home, please send a note to your child's teacher stating that he/she will not take the bus home that day.

The bus will stop at the following points:

_____ Victory Blvd. at Forest Ave.
_____ Bard and Oakland
_____ Bard and Myrtle
_____ Myrtle and Broad
_____ Broad and Seneca
_____ Seneca and Revere
_____ Revere and Brighton

It is important that parents emphasize that children must behave on the bus, while waiting for the bus, and on all lines. Children should be told to be careful when getting off the bus and when crossing the street.

Please complete this form, sign it, and return it to school.

I WISH MY CHILD TO RIDE THE SCHOOL BUS. I HAVE EXPLAINED TO MY CHILD THE IMPORTANCE OF PROPER BEHAVIOR ON THE BUS AND WHILE WAITING FOR IT.

Parent's signature:_____
Home address:_____
Home address:_____
Class:_____Child's name:_____
Bus stop he/she will use:_____

FIGURE 2-1: Bus Notice

How to best utilize auxiliary personnel

Secretary

Perhaps the most visible auxiliary staff member is the school secretary. She or he is an important link in the public relations chain. It is your job to keep the secretary aware of all school policies and practices. Now that the initial shock waves of the September

Dear Mrs._____,

Again on_____, your son (daughter)_____was disruptive on the school bus. This was reported to me by the driver and was investigated by_____.

As you know from our earlier conversations, this was not_____'s first incident on the bus. He (she) was warned by the teacher on duty and by me that this kind of misbehavior would not be tolerated. I spoke to you last week about the possibility of withdrawal of bus-riding privileges.

We are taking away this privilege for a period of five school days beginning_____. This is in accordance with school board policy (a copy of which is attached).

Withdrawal of bus riding privileges does not relieve the child or the parents of responsibility under the school attendance laws. The pupil must continue to attend school with the parents providing transportation.

If you have any questions, please call me at_____.

Sincerely,

FIGURE 2-2: Letter

opening are over you should meet regularly with the secretarial staff to discuss problems that have come up and anticipate future activities. Where there is more than one secretary, each should have fixed responsibilities determined as a result of cooperative planning with the supervisory staff. However, they should be trained to assume each other's duties and responsibilities in case of absence or emergency.

The principal should train the secretary and help with the upgrading of his or her skills. In case the regular secretary is absent, you should have available a checklist similar to the one in Figure 2-3.

The school secretary greets people—both in person and on the phone. It is important that he or she be pleasant at all times.

Custodian

An important factor in determining the success of any activity in the school building at any time is the efficient work of the custodian and his staff. The principal is responsible for the direction and control of the custodial staff. It is your responsibility to insure that a professional relationship exists between you and the

---

SUBSTITUTE SECRETARY CHECKLIST

___ 1. Regarding substitute teachers:
    a. Call substitute teachers for absent teachers.
    b. Obtain essential information from subs (social security number, salary step, license, etc.).
    c. Make appropriate entries in time book.
    d. Give the grade supervisors the names of subs in building.

___ 2. Consult the school calendar for the day's special activities: assemblies, class trips, reports due, etc.

___ 3. Study the District Calendar for reports due on the current day and in the near future; prepare reports.

___ 4. Check to see that bells have been turned on.

___ 5. Greet visitors warmly on the phone and in the office.

___ 6. Help get filing up to date.

___ 7. See which mimeographed notices have to get out.

___ 8. Attend to incoming mail:
    a. Give principal mail addressed to him or her.
    b. Route all mail opened and returned by the principal.
    c. Place in letter boxes mail addressed to teachers.

___ 9. Dispose of outgoing mail.

___10. Prepare a daily notation sheet for the regular secretary indicating work done.

___11. Follow the appropriate routine procedures for pupil admissions and discharges. Refer pupils who are admitted to the principal for placement.

___12. For teachers who have been absent, check on absence refund, non-attendance, or absence without pay forms.

___13. Complete accident reports, using the school format.

___14. Refer to the principal all requests for personnel data or information about pupils.

FIGURE 2-3: Substitute Secretary Checklist

custodian. Avoid getting overly familiar. October is a good time to talk about the approaching heating season. Discuss ways in which you can get the teachers to cooperate in conserving heat—for example, keeping windows closed and doors to the hallway open.

    The removal of snow is another topic you can explore with the custodian in October. Be sure that a relay system exists so that if schools are closed you can contact one another. Here are some key points that you the administrator should consider in your capacity as head of the school:

- Invite the custodian to participate in such activities as school assemblies and conferences dealing with matters of maintenance, safety, and vandalism.
- Keep the custodian informed of important changes in daily routines, such as schedules for Kindergarten or Senior Day, or Open School Week.
- Confer with the custodian in regard to setting up displays and planning special school events such as Book Fairs, science exhibits, cake sales, and bazaars.
- Alert the custodian to the need for training his helpers so that proper relationships with teachers, pupils, and parents may be established and maintained.
- Include the custodian's name and title on school organization sheets. Invite him to school functions.
- Confer with the custodian on all matters of plant improvement and daily maintenance.

Other Personnel

There is a host of other personnel connected with special services, such as the nurse, physician, attendance teacher, crossing guard, bus driver, lunchworker, and school aides. Because of his or her responsibility for matters involving every aspect of school life, the principal is properly concerned with the manner in which all personnel function within the school. He or she does not usually serve directly, however, as the supervisor of these personnel. If the principal finds it desirable to suggest changes or make recommendations involving these people, he or she should confer with them, and, if necessary, with their supervisors. October is a good time of year to get these matters straight. Later on in the year these things have become entrenched and are difficult to change.

You can make these personnel feel that they are an integral part of the staff and members of the working team by inviting them, if the occasion warrants it, to:

participate in staff conferences as guests and occasionally
    as speakers on appropriate topics;
speak at parents' meetings and pupil assemblies;
contribute to school and parent newspapers;
join in, with the faculty's approval, social activities
    planned by the staff.

What to do in case of a neighborhood disaster

While we hope this will never happen, every school must be prepared to disperse pupils in case some untoward event takes place. This is the best time of year to acquaint staff members with instructions as to how they are to proceed. You may want to meet with some grade leaders ahead of time to make refinements of this worksheet:

General Instructions

1. Teachers who are supervising classes—in classrooms, gymnasium, auditorium—are to *remain with pupils* wherever they are, while awaiting specific instructions. In the meantime do the following:

- a. Secure immediate attention and order.
- b. By calmness, self-assurance and good humor, reassure pupils that matters are under control.
- c. Start a game or song that will engage the children's interest and take their minds off the situation.
- d. Do NOT send pupils out of the room to office or elsewhere for ANY reason. Keep pupils with you and wait for further instructions.

2. Teachers who are out in yards, for yard duty or class outdoor period, are to bring pupils into line-up area AT ONCE and then to the closest shelter area within the school.

3. If disaster emergency occurs while teacher and class are in transit between classroom and some other part of the school building, go with pupils to official room if possible, or to assigned room shelter area.

4. During such emergency situation, adults may rush into the school to pick up children in order to take them home. Pupils may be released ONLY if you KNOW the adult is the parent or guardian of the child in question. A child may NOT be released to an adult who is not the child's parent or guardian unless release is authorized IN WRITING by the Main Office. Make a record, by name, of all pupils whom you have released.

5. If emergency occurs during time when pupils are arriving for the beginning of the session, the teachers will report to their classes in the area where pupils are assembled.

6. Handicapped children must be accounted for at all times. Do not leave physically handicapped children alone while you seek assistance.

Staff Assignments

1. The principal will take a post in the hallway outside the Main Office door to give direction, etc.

2. The assistant principal will take a post at main entrance of occupied floor above or below the one on which the principal is stationed. Supervise your floor, take any immediate action that may be necessary on the floor, and stand by for orders from the principal, via adult messenger. Take command of the school if the principal is absent or incapacitated.

3. Secretaries: Take post in the Main Office, unless ordered otherwise by person in charge of the school, to monitor telephone and radio broadcasts. Transmit messages to and from person in charge of school. Make office supply of first aid materials available as ordered. Refer to the person in charge of the school requests from adults to take pupils home. See to it that nobody uses the telephone for outgoing calls without authorization from the person in charge of the school. PHONES MUST BE KEPT OPEN.

4. Other teachers: Those teachers who are not on assignment with pupils (librarian, remedial, guidance) when emergency occurs, report to person in charge of school for assignment.

5. School nurse: Take post in Medical Office or room designated previously by the principal.

6. School aides: Report to person in charge of school for assignment.

7. Custodial staff: The custodian and his assistants shall secure operational plant factors for safety, i.e., water lines, gas lines, electricity, heating plant. Check all possible building damage factors. Report plant condition to person in charge of building. School matron should assist teacher with lowest grade.

8. Chain of command: The assistant principal will take charge of the school and make required decisions whenever the

principal is incapacitated or absent. Three teachers should be assigned to take charge in the event that all supervisors are absent.

9. Telephones: All lines are to be kept open. Keep incoming calls brief. Check bulletin board for emergency numbers.

Making the most of substitute teachers

October is the month when teachers begin to use their sick days and substitute teachers have to be called. Later on in mid-winter there will be days when many teachers may be out, so it is best to set up a procedure now for calling and deploying substitute teachers. We refer here to per diem substitutes who are called in for short durations, frequently just one day.

Here are some varied suggestions for dealing with some of the problems involving per diem substitute teachers:

- Ask your staff to call the school early in the morning if it is necessary for them to be absent.
- Have teachers call your secretary the night before if an absence is anticipated.
- Assign a member of your staff to be in school early to receive calls from absentees and to call substitute teachers.
- Discourage teachers from calling substitutes on their own.
- Give the per diem substitute the yard duty and other out-of-room assignments of the teacher whose class he or she is covering. When the sub cannot arrive on time, provision should be made to cover early morning assignments of absent teachers.
- Check regularly to see that every teacher has a list of routines for subs to follow inserted in his or her roll book. Some principals prefer to compose their own list of instructions, as shown below:

INFORMATION FOR SUBSTITUTES

1. Please record time of arrival and departure.
2. Study the Fire Drill and Shelter Area Drill notices in your room.
3. Call the roll at the beginning of each session and list the names of the absentees on a sheet of paper, dated and labeled. Place this sheet of paper in the roll book. Do *not* write in the roll book.
4. Attendance sheets are collected on_____at_____(A.M. or P.M.)
5. As far as possible, follow the plan in the teacher's plan book. It is to be found in the center drawer of the desk.
6. The teacher nearest to you is_____in Room____. He or she will be glad to give you help, if needed.

7. Should a serious situation arise, send for one of the supervisors.
8. The nearest women teachers' room is_____.
9. The nearest men teachers' room is_____.
10. Escort your class to the street level at dismissal time.
11. Hang up the keys in the office at the end of the day.
12. Your building assignment is_____.

Helping teachers identify special pupils

There has been a great deal of attention paid lately to pupils with developmental lags or special handicaps. But what is your school doing to identify and motivate intellectually gifted pupils? This is a good time of year to alert your teachers to seek out these special pupils. It is the administrators' responsibility to furnish the staff with objective criteria.

As you seek to identify the intellectually gifted, bear in mind that the child who is very proficient in one or two areas needs further study. Don't doubt your own observations or the results of tests if they show flashes of unusual intellectual ability in a child whose achievement record is low. Instead, consider that his or her background may be the cause of some cultural deprivation which can be compensated for in the school. The following list of identifying characteristics will help you to identify intellectually gifted children. Have each teacher make a class list of those pupils he or she wishes to recommend for special class placement or enrichment. After each name on the list have the teacher place the number of these characteristics he or she thinks apply:

1. Learns rapidly and easily.
2. Uses a lot of common sense and practical knowledge.
3. Knows about many things of which other children are unaware.
4. Reasons things out, thinks clearly, recognizes relationships.
5. Performs difficult mental tasks.
6. Retains what he has heard or read without much rote drill.
7. Uses a large number of words easily and accurately.
8. Can read books that are two or three years in advance of his grade.

It is best if you train your teachers to speak to you about these pupils before they talk to the parents. Too often a teacher will tell a parent that "your child is too smart for this class." The parent then storms into the office to seek a different placement. Frequently this is impossible, or, for some reason, inadvisable. Teachers should not recommend acceleration or special placement to parents without first talking to the administrator, who has a more global view of the school and may be aware of factors that would militate against such placement.

Teachers will also need your help in finding and placing special pupils who may be retarded, visually limited, aphasic, emotionally disturbed, brain injured, or physically handicapped. In most districts there are special clinical personnel who actually place the pupils in the special programs. But it is initially the alert teacher who brings such a child to your attention. It is a good idea early in the school year to devote a faculty conference to the recognition of those symptoms that may indicate that special class placement is indicated.

One gripe frequently heard from teachers is that they are never given the disposition of a case after they refer a child. Too often the classroom teacher is forgotten about in the scramble to get the parents' acceptance and the special placement indicated. To avoid this syndrome we are suggesting that a memo similar to the one in Figure 2-4 go to the referring teacher:

To: James Smith's teacher
From: Kent Clark, Guidance Counselor
Re: Special class placement   Date: October 14, 19__

   Thank you for referring James to this office for chronic inattention in the classroom. The physical work-up at the Central Hospital indicates that James has a 40% hearing loss due to a series of ear and throat infections.
   In a few weeks, Dr. Newman will be fitting James with a hearing aid. In the meantime your earlier suggestion to keep him seated near your desk in front of the room is the best way to compensate for this loss.
   Mrs. Smith was very grateful for the extra attention you were giving him, especially in regard to oral instructions.
   Thank you.

FIGURE 2-4: Memo

Guidelines for reporting pupil behavior

There are many occasions when it becomes necessary for your teachers to describe a child's behavior. It is your responsibility to train them to do this objectively and in sufficient detail to make the referral meaningful. Such referrals are needed when contacting an outside agency, when keeping anecdotal records, when preparing a report for possible suspension from school, or when reporting a child for special guidance help.

An examination of such recordings reveals a need for more specific description of behavior. This may result in better screening of referrals and perhaps speedier help for the child and family concerned.

In Column I of Figure 2-5 are listed samples taken from referral forms requesting agency help. In Column II there are suggestions that may help to give a better understanding of the nature of the problem.

BETTER GUIDANCE REFERRALS	
Column I	*Column II*
1. Poor attention span.	When doing what?
2. Fights with other children.	Any child? Only boys? What about? Where? In what situations?
3. Disruptive in class.	What does he do? What was class doing?
4. Temper-tantrums.	Provoked by what? When? How shown?
5. Uses bad language.	Swear words or obscenities? To whom? Under what conditions?
6. Not dependable.	What was expected of him that he failed to do?
7. Uncontrollable.	How shown? Who is involved?

FIGURE 2-5: Better Guidance Referrals

BETTER GUIDANCE REFERRALS (cont'd.)

Column I	*Column II*
8. Needs constant attention.	How does he seek it? From whom? What does he do when he can't get it?
9. Does not get along with teachers.	How shown? How does he behave?
10. Lazy.	What does he do when he is not doing his work? Is it shown during some activities and not others?
11. Resentful.	What does he resent? How shown? Are adults or peers involved?
12. Extremely restless.	What does he do? When? Always?
13. Unresponsive.	To what is he not responding? How is it manifested?
14. Bizarre behavior.	What does he do that seems strange? How shown?
15. Shy.	In what situations? How shown? In relationship to whom?
16. Withdrawn.	Do not confuse with shyness. Is child unable to take part in any activities? Does child relate to no one? Does he seem preoccupied with own thoughts?
17. Uncooperative.	What does he refuse to do? In what situation?
18. Dominates the group.	How? Mental or physical?
19. Parent uncooperative.	How does parent see the problem? How does the parent feel about agency help?
20. Does not respond to assistance.	What has been tried? What does he react to?

FIGURE 2-5: Better Guidance Referrals (continued)

GENERAL RULES FOR AGENCY REFERRALS

1. Do not refer cases already active in an agency.
2. Do not withhold pertinent information.
3. Be sure forms are signed by the principal.
4. Include anecdotal records.
5. When there is more than one recorded I.Q., list all.
6. When making a retarded child referral, indicate if there is also a behavior problem.
7. Discuss with the parent the fact that a referral is indicated and prepare the parent for accepting such help.
8. Cover each item on the referral form.
9. Be specific.
10. Be objective.
11. Do not diagnose.
12. Use factual rather than judgmental statements.
13. Use positive as well as negative aspect of child's behavior.
14. Consult health card and include information source.

October observations

This October make it your resolve not to be so thin skined that every criticism will put you in a dither. The very nature of your role puts you in a visible and vulnerable position. The community will know things about you whether you wish them to or not. Certainly, some secrets can be kept, and rightfully so, but many aspects of one's personality and way of operating cannot be hidden, no matter how skillful the attempt to do so.

Teachers and students will react to the principal's smile, frown, clothing style, hairstyle, glasses, automobile, and vocabulary. The principal must realize that no matter how impeccable his or her dress or behavior someone will scoff at his or her mannerisms, conduct, or appearance.

If you do not have enough confidence in yourself to weather the storm of criticism, subtle or overt, you will be an unhappy person in today's schools. Ten or more years ago, the school administrator could have been detached from staff or pupils. This is no longer possible. Much of this criticism is unjustified in the first place. But today's mores insist that people be critical of those in authority, whether justifiably so or not.

You have little choice but to realize that you will be a convenient target for criticism that can come at any time from any source and from any direction. To the degree that you can protect your flanks successfully, you will be able to handle the criticism without loss of patience and without loss of self-esteem. However, to the degree that the criticism renders you ineffective, you will be an easy target.

The realization that criticism is inevitable in your job is difficult enough. The real test of your self-confidence is your ability to handle criticism that you consider unfair, unfounded, and unnecessary, especially from those whom you have trusted or befriended. This can be a teacher's union chapter chairman, PTA official, district office coordinator, or intermediate supervisor.

As principal you cannot remain indifferent to this major problem of criticism. No amount of advice can save you from critical attacks. Advice can only serve to keep you ever vigilant so that you can overcome the tendency to be super-sensitive to whatever your critics say.

This does not mean that the criticism should be ignored. No one is above criticism, not even those elected to high office. The principal cannot react to every critical statement, but certainly you should take into consideration what your critics are saying.

How you can set up an after-school program

With the various budgetary cutbacks in recent years it is not always possible to fund an after-school program with tax-levy monies. This should not stop you from having a full and varied after-school program paid for on a self-sustaining basis. That is, you charge a nominal fee of $10.00 for ten sessions. This money is used primarily to pay the teachers' hourly salaries, with some money spent on supplies that are not available from the regular day school program. For example: 18 pupils sign up for Woodworking. Their fees come to $18.00 per session. The teacher is paid $11.00 per session. That leaves $7.00 per session or $70.00 per course left over. This surplus can pay for some materials or partial scholarships or to cover some other course with a smaller register. It is important to offer those courses that your particular pupil population is interested in. The best way to ascertain this is to send home a flyer describing the program and fee schedule and ask parents and pupils to indicate which courses and which afternoon they are interested in. From the responses to the flyers you can make your course offering list and hire the teachers. Wherever possible try to get teachers from your school. This will avoid the problem of having teachers arrive late and will boost morale. You owe it to your pupils and parents to hire only the best qualified teachers, however. After doing that you can send home the reminder shown in Figure 2-6.

When these slips have been returned with checks you will know just where you stand. You may determine ahead of time that "13" will represent your cut-off. Fewer than 13 pupils will not pay for the course. If you have an overage in some other offering you may be able to "carry" the smaller register. Involve one or two parents in helping you register the pupils and in assisting the teachers after school. A parent with bookkeeping skills can take care of the payroll under your direction.

Handling absence for religious observance

The school calendar contains many different kinds of "off" days. There are legal holidays when the buildings are closed. Then there are legal holidays when some districts hold classes, such as Election Day, Lincoln's Birthday and Washington's Birthday. In the area of religious holidays there are even more gray areas. Jewish children observe their New Year on holidays that begin with Rosh Hashana and end with Yom Kippur. Like all Jewish holidays and also some Christian holidays, such as Easter, they follow a lunar calendar and fall on different dates each year. Yom Kippur may occur in September or October, and on a weekend or during the week.

Greek, Russian and other Eastern Orthodox Churches celebrate familiar religious holidays but do so on days different from those of Roman Catholic and Protestant churches. It is important that you acquaint your teachers with the different holidays and that you ask them to excuse their pupils who are absent for purposes of celebrating their holiday.

Commissioners of Education have recognized the following days of religious observance, whenever they fall on a day when

October 31, 197

Dear Parents:

Your response to our letter concerning the After-School Enrichment Center has been most encouraging. We are now ready to
register your child for the course of your choice. Registration will
take place on Monday and Wednesday (November 3 and 5) in the
Lunchroom, at 3:15 P.M. Please send your youngster with the tear-
off slip below and check for $10.00 (NO CASH, PLEASE), payable
to "P.S. 45 A.S.E.C." you must send in or bring in *this* slip with a
check. The earlier notice was merely a survey to see which courses
you were interested in.

Courses will be held on Thursday afternoons from 3:15 to 4:15
P.M. for ten weeks (November 6 through January 29). We reserve the
right to cancel a course if registration does not warrant its inclusion.

Please choose from this list:

COURSE		*ELIGIBILITY*
Pre-kindergarten	_____	(Pupils who will be attending P.S. 45 Kindergarten next year.)
Sports Skills	_____	Grades 3-5
Dance	_____	Grades 2-5
Woodworking	_____	Grades 3-5
Needlework	_____	Grades 2-5
Photography	_____	Grades 3-5
Playacting	_____	Grades 3-5
Art	_____	Grades 1-5

- -

Tear off and return to school

P.S. 45 A.S.E.C.
Course:_____
Pupil's Name:_____ Class:_____
Address:_____Phone:_____

FIGURE 2-6: Reminder Letter

school is in session. Pupils are excused on these days upon prior
written request of the parents or guardians. These days are not

legal holidays. The attendance register should be maintained as on other days of the session.

In order to provide you with a concrete example, Figure 2-7 presents a typical school year. Do remember that while these holidays are observed each year, the calendar dates will vary for many of them.

DAYS OF RELIGIOUS OBSERVANCE

September	Feast of the Elevation of the Cross **
	Rosh Hashana (Jewish New Year) *
	Yom Kippur*
	Sukkoth*
November 1	Feast of All Saints
December 8	Feast of the Immaculate Conception
25	Christmas
January 1	Feast of the Circumcision
1	Feast of Mary
6	Feast of the Epiphany**
7	Christmas**
19	Feast of the Epiphany***
Feb. or Mar.	Ash Wednesday
March	Annunciation
Mar. or Apr.	Passover
	Holy Thursday
	Good Friday
	Easter
May	Feast of the Ascension
	Shabuoth

*September or October
**Greek Orthodox Celebration
***Eastern Orthodox Celebration

FIGURE 2-7: Religious Observance

Planning a Columbus Day Parade

One of the earliest celebrations in the school year is Columbus Day. If your school has a sizable Italo-American population, this holiday takes on even more meaning. Teachers are quite creative in planning individual classroom activities, such as puppet shows, dioramas, model ships, etc. An excellent school-wide activity is a Columbus Day parade. Everyone loves a parade, and the many preparations needed are rewarded by the enjoyment shared by all.

To help you plan the parade we suggest the following checklist:

1. Permits—Many permits are needed in large cities. Check with the Police Department.
2. Parade Route—Don't fail to consider exploring new parade routes. Often, if a particular street has been consistently bypassed for a more popular thoroughfare, merchants or street associations of the neglected route are more than happy to support your efforts.
3. Duration—Decide early how long the parade will run. This is one of the first questions you'll be asked when you apply for permits. A parade should last only as long as the fun lasts. There is nothing exciting about watching tired children shuffle by.
4. Traffic Control—While this is an item for the police, you will have to arrange a smooth delivery and pickup service for the band and other groups of pupils.
5. Program—The heart of the parade is the program or theme you follow. An essential element is music. You can augment the school band and/or glee club with a Knights of Columbus band. Most organizations with bands are happy to participate, since this is the kind of event they've practiced all year for. You may want to include a colorful float. Your parade should have at least one color guard heading the procession with the American Flag and followed by state, school, or the Italian flag.
6. Marchers—In addition your pupils, include military units, verterans' groups, Scouts, and the PTA.

Sample conference notes

FACULTY CONFERENCE

Monday, October 2, 19___

I.   Acknowledgment.
      1.1   We're off to a good start, thanks to your hard work and cooperation. The bus service should smooth out by next

week. Continue to report to the office the number of pupils who arrive after the nine o'clock bell.

II. Administrative Items.

2.1 Attendance Period: The second attendance period ends October 31. Total days this period—21. Total days to date—34.

2.2 Salary Credit: Please see school secretary if you did not receive your increment credit on your last check.

2.3 Bulletin Boards: Our bulletin boards have many fine displays of pupils' work. Please make it a point to label your hall bulletin boards as to class.

2.4 Report Cards: Distribution day is November 7. Be sure to send cards to grade supervisor on November 5.

2.5 Notices: It has come to our attention that some notices have not gone home. Be sure to distribute these the day they are received. Have the children put them in their notebooks so they don't forget to give them to their parents.

2.6 Use of Lavatories: In general, pupils should not have to leave the room before 10 A.M., after 11:30 A.M., before 1:30 P.M., or after 2:30 P.M. Remind pupils to sign out-of-room book provided for that purpose.

2.7 Monitors: Remember to alternate monitors so that the same children are not out of the room too often and so that all will have a chance to serve.

2.8 Door Sign: If you do not already have one, please make a sign that indicates where your class has gone when you are not in the room.

2.9 Building Security: In the event an intruder gets into the building, the staff will be code alerted over the Public Address system by the statement that "Mrs. Hamilton should report to_____" (area where intruder was seen).

III. Supervision and Improvement of Instruction.

3.1 Early Starts: Please get into active teaching of lessons by 9 A.M. Opening exercises and collections should be out of the way by that time—except possibly in a few of the lower grade classes.

3.2 Grade Conferences: Brief report by each grade leader.

3.3   Stress the Positive: Stress the positive whenever you can. Avoid giving demerits to those who don't or can't. Instead, *do* give recognition in various ways to those who *do*—e.g., in your health inspection, praise the pupils who do meet your standards. The non-conformists will feel left out and will usually come around.

IV.   Open School Week.

This will be from October 23 through October 26. The theme this year is "Get Involved." Begin now to prepare folders of pupil work. Check to see that many different pupils have work displayed on classroom corkboards.

Role Playing: Parents and teacher at Open School Night—
First parent: Mrs. Flynn
Second parent: Miss Rucci
Third parent: Mr. Aleman

Next conference: Monday, November 19

From the Principal's Desk

In most schools the parents' organization has some kind of monthly newsletter in which they ask the principal to write a message each month. For October we suggest the theme, "Halloween—Time for Fun and Safety."

Halloween is a special day for children. It is a day they get to dress up in a variety of costumes and take to the streets, knocking on doors in search of special treats.

Traditionally, if a child does not receive a treat, he will play a trick. But in recent years, an increasing number of "tricks" have been played by adults on children, sometimes with tragic results.

Parents should take precautions against possible dangers their children may be exposed to. In the interest of encouraging wholesome fun along with safety, I am suggesting the following:

● A responsible adult should accompany all young children in their rounds, preferably before nightfall. If the rounds take place after dark, flashlights are recommended.

● Doorbell ringing should be limited to homes that are well lighted in anticipation of visits by little goblins and ghosts.

● Care should be taken to use sidewalks and avoid lawns where there may be objects to trip over.

- Stay away from the homes of known neighborhood cranks, who are the most likely to be planning some "tricks" of their own.
- Always cross streets at intersections after carefully looking both ways.
- Children should be forbidden to eat any gifts of food until they have returned home. All the treats should be carefully inspected, and fruit cut into small pieces, to make sure they do not harbor harmful objects. Candy that is broken, unwrapped, or wrapped loosely should be discarded. Popcorn in any form is a "no-no."
- Costumes should be made or bought with care. Make sure they are flame-retardant without loose folds to trip over. Reflective tape should be applied so an oncoming automobile will pick up the presence of a pint-sized witch, pirate, or clown.
- Masks can be hazardous because they limit a child's vision. A suggested substitute is colorful makeup based on a child's own design of how he or she wants to be disguised.
- Parents should use care in lighting jack-o-lanterns with candles. They should be out of the reach of children.

By following these simple safety suggestions we can make sure that our children enjoy a colorful Halloween without any untoward event marring their fun.

OCTOBER CURRICULUM CALENDAR

United Nations Week and UNICEF Day. Focus on things international. Emphasize the concept of world citizenship. Point out not only cultural differences but also the ways we are all alike regardless of nationality.

Fire Prevention Week. Remind pupils that fire drills are important not only in school but at home, too. Ask them to talk with their families about what to do in case of a fire and to plan a family fire drill.

Columbus Day. What would Columbus' reaction be if he landed in the New World this year instead of in 1492? What do you think would impress him most in the way we live today? Which form of transportation would fascinate him the most?

William Penn. The founder of Pennsylvania was born on October 14, 1644. As a Quaker he was put in prison three times for writing and preaching. He came to the colonies in search of religious freedom. What problems did he encounter?

Daylight Saving Time. D.S.T. ends at 2 A.M. on the last Sunday of this month and Standard Time resumes. What does the sun have to do with the length of daylight?

National Magic Day. This is observed on the anniversary of the death of Harry Houdini on October 31, 1926. Invite a local magician to dazzle children with mind-boggling feats.

Chapter 3

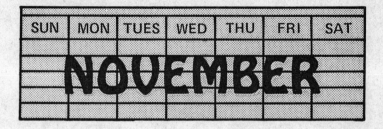

Improving Parent-Teacher Conferences

This is the month when conferences are held between parents and teachers. While this can be a very valuable experience for both parties, too often it becomes a threatening encounter for one or both sides. For some parents a visit to school brings back unpleasant memories of their own unsatisfactory school experiences. For some teachers who are not very secure in their own position or who are in awe of the parents of their pupils, this is a time to overreact, withdraw, or become unintentionally pretentious.

You as the principal can avoid parent complaints or teacher dissatisfaction by sending a letter out to all the parents prior to the parent-teacher conferences. A letter like the one shown in Figure 3-1 will give some structure to the interview and will provide a focus for mutually rewarding dialogue:

Successful parent-teacher conferences depend on the use of good interviewing techniques on the part of the teachers. A good interview can build wholesome home-school ties. Listed below are pointers for your teachers to be aware of in preparing for, conducting, and following up an interview. You may want to reproduce these in your conference notes or discuss them when meeting with individual teachers.

1. Do not sit behind your desk. It is far easier to build a cooperative, workable relationship if you are seated alongside the

Dear Parents:

Next Tuesday afternoon our school will be holding parent-teacher interviews. In order to make your conference a profitable one, we would like to suggest some things you might want to ask about and some things you might want to tell the teacher.

You may want to ask the teacher:

1. Does my child participate in classroom activities?
2. Does he/she join in discussions or make suggestions?
3. Does my child show self-control in school situations?
4. How does my child get along with the other children?
5. Does he/she relate well to the teacher and other adults?
6. Can my child handle the learning materials of the grade (textbooks, reference books, science materials, gym equipment)?
7. Does he/she seem to enjoy reading during his/her spare time?
8. Is his/her comprehension suitable to his/her grade level?
9. How does my child read orally? Does he/she know the number facts?
10. Can he/she express his/her thoughts and ideas clearly?
11. How is his/her written communication?
12. Does my child seem happy in school? Is he/she accepted by the other children?

You may want to tell the teacher:

1. Which school activities your child talks about at home.
2. What responsibilities your child handles at home.
3. If anything has happened lately at home that might affect your child's performance at school.
4. Which classmates your child sees at home.
5. What are some of your child's favorite activities outside of school.
6. How you discipline your child at home.
7. What are your child's strengths and weaknesses.

Sharing information about your child with his/her teacher will enable us to provide a learning program that will best meet the needs of your child.

Thank you for your cooperation. Remember—the conference times are between 1:00 P.M. and 4:00 P.M.

Sincerely,_____
                          Principal

FIGURE 3-1: Parent-Teacher Conference Letter

parent. Behind the desk, the teacher is in a position of authority, not partnership.

2. Prior to the actual interview, assemble all the materials you need, such as marking books, rating sheets, tests, results, and samples of class work.

3. Welcome all the parents warmly. Make them feel at ease and secure. Many parents, when they enter a school building, feel uneasy, guilty, timid, threatened, or a failure. These are the feelings they had in school.

4. Open the interview on a positive note. Use expressions of approval, praise, or satisfaction for something the child can do well or has experienced with success.

5. Do NOT at any time refer to the child as a "liar," "stupid," "dumb," "delinquent," or "lazy." Describe some of the things the child does and let the parents come to their own conclusions: "John does not finish his work," or "Mary acts as though she doesn't hear any instructions."

6. Accept the parent and his/her explanations without showing surprise or disapproval. If you will do this, you will get a true and honest picture of the parent's feelings and attitudes.

7. Keep aware of the time. Other parents will be waiting to talk to you. If you need more time, schedule another appointment.

8. End the interview on a positive note. Summarize the highlights for the parent or state a positive plan for cooperative action between the school and the home.

9. By all means be sympathetic, but keep in mind that you are not a marriage counselor, psychologist, or faith healer. Keep the interview focused on the child and the school. Do not encourage parents to talk about their mates or their ailments.

10. Listen to the parent. Remember that an interview is a two-way conversation. It is not merely a chance for you to show the parent how smart you are. Behind every halting or inarticulate parent is a caring, experienced adult who has learned a thing or two about life along the way.

Insuring a successful Open School Week

Careful planning is an ingredient of almost every school activity, and Open School Week is no exception. You as the school administrator cannot assume that just because a teacher has been in your school or your school district for a number of years, he or she is ready for so important an event as Open School Week. It is your responsibility to prepare the staff as well as invite the parents at least two weeks ahead of the date. It is usually observed nationwide at the same time.

Start your plan by taking a look at your school plant from the eyes of a parent-visitor. Take a walk with your custodian through your building and around it. Is there some eyesore that you shut out of your vision because you see it every day that can be removed or screened from view? Are there some areas of graffiti that can be covered over with a little paint? Take a critical look at your hall bulletin boards. Do they look motheaten and tired? Do they display pupil work or tired posters saved by teachers from year to year?

Parent-visitors invariably have occasion to use the pupil washrooms. What do yours look like? What suggestions does your custodian have for sprucing them up? Since it is early in the year, perhaps a good start will motivate the pupils to keep them looking good.

Visit every classroom. Inspect the classroom bulletin boards. Are they current? Are charts, pictures, and test papers in good condition? What about the book cases and pupil desks—are they cluttered or neat? Does the teacher's desk provide a good example for the pupils to follow? Check to see that no basins or rags are on radiators or anywhere in sight. Blackboards and ledges should be cleaned regularly. Encourage your teachers to have on the classroom door, welcoming the parents, a poster made by a pupil.

Train your teachers to have a folder or envelope of pupil work for every child in the room. These should be available for parental inspection.

Remind your staff that they should keep to their regular routine as much as possible during Open School Week. The parents should be able to see a typical school day to the extent that this is possible with visitors coming and leaving. Teachers should be cautioned to continue with their lessons and not stop to talk to individual parents. Ask your teachers to have a sign-in sheet in the back of the room so that you can have a record of the parents who visited the school.

This is a good time to have members of the PTA sit at a table in the lobby and direct visitors to the appropriate room. They may want to take advantage of this opportunity to enroll parents in the

PTA. You may choose instead to have pupil hosts and hostesses who can direct parents to different rooms in the building.

Since some parents will have children in different grades within the school, you may want to schedule certain grades for certain days of the week. In this way parents will be able to spend a reasonable amount of time in each child's room without the temptation to rush out and go into another child's room. For parents who have taken one day off from work to visit all of their children's rooms, this plan will not work.

American Education Week is the formal name for Open School Week, and in most school districts the building is "open" to visitors. In some school districts this necessitates increased security to make sure that no undesirable outsiders come into the building. As a precaution, you may want to have your visitors sign a book.

Still other school districts have used this week as an opportunity to take the school into the open—to send the school into the community where it can get the greatest possible exposure. In the modern suburb this might be the shopping center; in the inner city it might be a busy shopping street. The shopping center can become a showcase for some elements of a school program. Obviously you couldn't show the public a remedial reading lesson in such a setting but you could give a big boost to the school band, gymnasts, science fair winners, artists, glee club, teams, cheerleaders, or newspaper or magazine staffs. The home economics club could hold a fashion show, or the industrial arts group could sell ceramic or wood projects.

You won't have much difficulty convincing the manager of a shopping center that the school has something to offer. Designate one member of the school staff to act as liaison person with the center. If it's a one-school project, it should be a teacher or administrator; if several schools are involved, someone from the central office should coordinate things. Experienced principals tell us that such details as these must be worked out in advance: exact locations for the delivery of materials, a timetable for transporting both personnel and materials, arranging such things as the loan of pianos to accompany musical groups, providing for public address systems, and insuring that enough extension cords are available for lights.

If you plan this activity sufficiently in advance, you can count on the merchants to publicize the events in their newspaper, radio and TV advertisements and in their direct-mail flyers. Both the school and the storekeepers should alert the media through news releases. Planning ahead will make the program come off as a headliner rather than as an afterthought. In addition, more parents and community people will see the school program painlessly than can be expected if you wait for them to come to school. Of course, you can reach the greatest audience by combining the traditional Open School Week with a shopping center display at a later date.

　　We have found that a letter inviting parents to come to school is made more effective if you have a "tear off" at the bottom. A sample of such a letter is given in Figure 3-2.

Dear Parents:

　　You are cordially invited to visit your child's class during Open School Week, November 17 through November 21. The theme for this year is "Our Future Is in Our Schools." You are welcome whenever you can come during this week. No pass is required at this time.

　　Since this visit is designed to let you see your child and his/her classmates at work, the teacher has been requested *not* to engage in conversation with any parent during this visit. Please cooperate by entering the classroom quietly and by taking a place at the back of the room. Do not distract the class and teacher by walking around to inspect displays or to talk to a child.

　　The opportunity to inspect your child's work, to meet the teacher, and to discuss your child's progress will be given on two other dates this month. A special notice will be sent to you regarding these dates.

　　I sincerely hope that you will avail yourselves of the opportunity to visit and acquaint yourself with your child's work in school.

Sincerely yours,
Marion Hayes
Principal

　　Please tear off and return to your child's teacher.

　　I have received the notice dated November 6th regarding Open School Week and have made note of the contents.

| Child's Name | Class | Parent's Signature |

FIGURE 3-2

Encourage your teachers to distribute these notices early enough for parents to make plans to come to the school during Open School Week. One problem that seems difficult to resolve is what visiting parents should do about pre-school children. Not all mothers can leave them at home. Most of these very young children pose a noise problem when they visit the school. One solution attempted in many schools is to have some PTA volunteers take over an empty classroom and act as babysitters for the period of time that the mothers are in the building. If you arbitrarily tell parents to leave the pre-school children at home, you may in effect be telling them to stay home.

Keep a notebook of Open School activities you tried this year with some brief comments on what worked and what did not. It needn't be elaborate; it doesn't even have to be intelligible to anyone else. But for you, as you plan your Open School events in future years, it will be of great value, for it will help you not to make your first year's mistakes *every* year.

How to integrate the curriculum with a school-wide activity

Every school can benefit from some universal activity that captures the imagination and interest of every student regardless of grade or general ability level. During the month of November an obvious choice, and one that works well especially on the junior high school level, is a mock election.

For the last few weeks the pupils have been bombarded at home by campaign literature and television appearances of political candidates. They may have heard family members talking about the candidate they favor. Rather than ignore this topical news event that is building in interest, you can capitalize upon it for your school.

If this is an off-year election with candidates running for many different offices, it is best if the school zeroes in on just the major seats being filled. Other offices should be reviewed casually. Frequently school buildings are used as polling stations, and this heightens pupil interest. You may be able to set up poll booths of your own. Of course, you will hold this mock election sufficiently before the real election so that your results can be tabulated and announced prior to the real election.

Virtually all of your teachers will become involved. Industrial arts teachers will guide students in the construction of ballot boxes and voting booths. Art teachers will devote class time to the drawing of posters. Foreign language teachers will help pupils translate campaign literature into other languages.

Social studies teachers have the obvious opportunity to center their lessons on the issues and personalities of the campaign. They should describe the duties of each office and be scrupulous in providing equal time and not favoring any one candidate.

Math teachers have an interesting problem to pose in a presidential election year: How is it possible for a candidate to win the popular vote, yet still lose the election? There are many math implications in the voting process in every election.

Language arts teachers may ask pupils to write election speeches or to report on those that have been heard or read. Tape recordings of classroom debates stimulate good speech patterns. Children should be encouraged to interview others in and out of school on campaign issues, thus developing their interview techniques.

Results of the election in school are tabulated and publicized. Schools doing this over a period of years begin to see their results studied as a trend for the actual election.

What if two or more classes want to use the auditorium at the same time? Use a "Use of Auditorium" form such as the one shown in Figure 3-3 to avoid conflicts.

Focusing on the "Discovery of Puerto Rico Week"

The week of November 17 is a time of celebration for pupils whose parents have come from this Caribbean island. Puerto Rican Discovery Day marks the beginning of a week-long recognition of the rich cultural heritage that characterizes the history of the Puerto Rican people. The language, culture, customs, mores of the Puerto Rican people have imparted their special color and texture to our country and particularly to those large urban centers to which most of these people migrated. Bilingual and bicultural programs have been designed to develop skilled graduates whose cultural and ethnic identity remains intact while they learn skills and acquire the tools that will make it possible for them to function

Public School 45, District 5
The John Tyler School

Mr. Francis Jones, Principal

USE OF AUDITORIUM

DATE DAY	9:05 to 9:50	9:55 to 10:40	10:45 to 11:00	11:30 to 12:00	12:00 to 1:00	1:20 to 2:05	2:05 to 2:50	2:50 to 3:30
MON					L			Chorus Practice
TUE	Upper Assembly				U	Band	Band Band	Band
WED					N		Lower Assembly	
THUR				Chorus Practice	C			Club Hour
FRI	Band	Band Band	Band		H	Cleaning by custodian		

FIGURE 3-3

at their own highest level. Impress upon your staff the importance of preserving the heritage and background that these pupils bring to the mainland.

Lifting the burden of the language barrier is the first step toward full bilingual-bicultural education. It will embrace and support children of Puerto Rican heritage whose dominant language is Spanish, and help make the transition from one school system to another as non-threatening and as reassuring as possible. Through bilingual educational programs, Spanish-speaking children will become our advantaged children. Their bilingualism can become an asset rather than a deficit, a distinction rather than a stigma. The attitude that you and your staff display toward these children and their parents will make the difference. Mainland children will be enriched by a study of the contributions of different cultural strains to our country. This week is a good opportunity to launch such a study of cultural diversity.

How to reward positive pupil behavior

Teachers on every school level are concerned with student misbehavior—from minor disruptions of school routine to actual assaults on persons. Many teachers cite discipline problems as the reason for their leaving the profession.

Scientists studying human behavior have found that behavior that is rewarded tends to be repeated; behavior that is not rewarded is not likely to be repeated. This approach is also called positive feedback, behavior modification, reinforcement theory of learning. No matter what you call it, there are case studies to show that when it is applied correctly, it works!

Your teachers probably have read about behavior modi-fication or have had some course work in it. A little knowledge about any learning theory is hardly enough to make you want to adopt it school-wide. There are some occasions when such a practice could backfire. Based on the experience of many others, we are giving you some caveats here:

The middle schools and elementary schools are the best places to adapt these theories. Senior high school students are usually more "rewarded" by the approval of their peers than by the ap-proval or other rewards given by teachers.

The more quickly the reinforcement follows the act, the more effective it will be.

Don't expect instant results. There should be some behavior improvement in three or four days if you have been consistent in your rewarding of a child's good behavior.

Don't start with the idea of changing all of a child's inappropriate behavior at once. Behavior modification works best when you concentrate on one disruptive activity at a time (pushing on line, shouting out answers, or fighting, for example).

All children do not respond to the same rewards or reinforcements. One pupil may beam with pleasure when you say "I'm proud of you," while another may cringe at the same words. What you may see as a reward (verbal praise before the class) may actually embarrass a child before his age mates.

You must vary the kinds of rewards you use, or they'll get stale and lose their impact.

In a nutshell, using the behavior modification method you no longer try to catch children doing something bad. You try to catch them doing something good. And each time you do, you reward them for it. *Immediately*. This is the crux of the method.

Tips on handling the disruptive child

November is the month when discipline problems come into full bloom. It is no longer the beginning of the term and the Christmas vacation is not yet in sight. If you are the person who handles most of the discipline cases you probably are already using some kind of referral card or other method of formalizing the flow of misbehaving pupils from the classroom to your office.

The referral form contains all important information, such as student's name, teacher's name, date of offense, time, place, and a brief description of the incident. If this is not the first offense the teacher should describe the previous action taken. This card should be sent in as soon after the offense as possible, but it should not be filled out during class time. It is important that teachers know that they may use any available paper if no cards are handy. Red tape and procedures must not prevent a report from being written while the incident is fresh in the teacher's mind. Even a one-day delay can obscure the facts and make the punishment less effective.

Keeping pupils in after school in a detention room or the administrator's office is an age-old practice that works if it is not over-utilized. Since many of your pupils are dependent on the school bus to get home, you may have to have a 24-hour delay in serving their detention. In the secondary school where pupils may have a part-time job after school you may have to allow a 48-hour delay so that detainees can arrange matters with their employers. Beyond that time, work does not excuse a pupil from detention.

One of the most effective and positive ways to help a pupil improve his behavior is to furnish the parents with biweekly reports. As the administrator, you would want to have accurate up-to-date information to forward to the home. A sample form is shown in Figure 3-4.

DEAN'S OFFICE REQUEST FOR PUPIL INFORMATION

Pupil's
Name:_____ Class:_____ Date:_____
Any absences this week?
General behavior:
Was student prepared?
Relationships with peers:
Was he respectful to adults?
Any quiz or test marks this week?
Any attitudinal changes noted?

FIGURE 3-4

Please be aware of the fact that these reports from teachers to you the administrator are privileged and written for your eyes only. Do not yield to the temptation of merely photocopying them and forwarding them to the parent. It is your responsibility to paraphrase them and collate the comments of all the teachers. Not to do this would result in several bad situations: (1) teachers may not agree on a youngster's behavior in a given week and the parent may then pit one teacher against another; (2) a teacher may include information about another pupil in the report, and this should not go home; (3) occasionally a teacher may display poor judgment or sound harsh in a report to you, and this should not go home. You are able to perceive a more global view and then relay an accurate picture to the parents. This editing should not take much time and the results will prove to be worthwhile.

Some pupils who display self-control in the classroom of an elementary school become behavior problems when in the lunchroom. In such cases you should send home a letter like the one in Figure 3-5.

Dear Mrs. Mather:

Your son, Elliot, of Class 5-303, has been barred from eating in the lunchroom for a week beginning November 2nd because his behavior is endangering the safety of the other children.

Please make arrangements for him to eat elsewhere or he will be placed in a special room for the entire lunch period.

Since he will not be permitted to enter the lunchroom, it will be necessary for you to provide a cold lunch for him.

Please detach and return the bottom part of this letter. Also, include your phone number since we were not able to reach you on the telephone.

> Very truly yours,
>
> Carl Linton
> Principal

_ _

Dear Mr. Linton:

I have read your letter regarding my son's/daughter's lunchroom behavior. I understand he/she must not eat in the lunchroom during the week of_____.

> _____
> Parent's Signature

FIGURE 3-5

Orienting pupils to a large school

The sheer size of many large urban high schools has created problems of anonymity. Part of our ongoing task as administrators is to break down this anonymity and personalize, as far as possible, the educational environment. The tremendous size of incoming classes each year also inhibits the process of communication. As a result school administrators of large schools across the country have reported the following situations:

1. Most incoming pupils do not fully participate in the life of the school until their second or third year of high school.

2. Participation in co-curricular activities is limited because pupils are not aware of the full spectrum of activities. If they are aware of activities they don't know whom to see or how to join.

3. Pupils, particularly those least able to suffer loss of instruction, carry incorrect programs, only to discover the errors too late.

4. Large numbers of pupils lack knowledge of services available to them in their high school. Very often this is true of teachers as well.

5. Most pupils have never had a complete picture of the curricular offerings available to them, nor are they aware of the process of electing alternative subjects.

6. Misinformation, apathy, and misunderstanding result from such pupil ignorance, with consequences harmful both to the individual student and to the tone of the school.

One way of dealing with these problems is to utilize a team approach, as was done at Lafayette High School in Brooklyn. They had become dissatisfied with their existing method of orientation, which had consisted of visits to feeding junior high schools, large orientation assemblies in the fall, and dissemination of information to pupils via the official class, bulletins, and loudspeaker announcements.

After meetings with the staff they decided to pilot a series of mini-orientation conferences utilizing a team approach. The main features of the conference would be:

1. Limiting the number of pupils to about 100 or three subject classes.

2. The presentation of several orientation conferences rather than one large-group assembly.

3. Allowing time for pupil questions and interaction with the team.

4. Using the conferences to poll pupil preferences regarding co-curricular activities.

5. The use of orientation teams consisting of faculty and students representing varying points of view with regard to school life.

6. Reaching every incoming pupil by the end of November.

In the past, the orientation of new pupils had largely been the responsibility of guidance counselors or grade advisers. Lafayette High School replaced them with a team approach utilizing classroom teachers, thus broadening the definition or orientation and providing for more varied input into the process. The three teams were made up as follows:

Team A

Foreign Language Chairman
Guidance Counselor
Dean of Boys
Teacher
3 students

Team B

Chairman of Business Subjects
Guidance Counselor
Dean of Girls
Teacher
3 students

Team C

Health Education Chairman
Guidance Counselor
2 teachers
3 students

They decided to reach all the incoming pupils through the science classes. Each team was assigned one third of the total number of these subject classes (about 15 classes per team) and, after consultation with the chairman of the science department, communicated directly with the science teachers. Team A worked periods 7 and 9; Team B worked periods 6, 8 and 10; Team C worked periods 4, 6 and 11. They found the optimum group size to be three subject classes (about 90-100 pupils). This number allowed them to move rapidly and yet work with manageable groups. They tried to avoid the vastness of the auditorium and used music rooms whenever possible; these rooms seat 100 pupils.

Sample conference notes

STAFF CONFERENCE

Monday, November 19, 19___

In the little world in which children have their existence, whosover brings them up, there is nothing so finely perceived and so finely felt as injustice.

—Charles Dickens

I.   Administrative Notes.

1.1   Attendance Period: Third attendance period ends November 30. Total days this period—19. Total days to date—53.

1.2   Health Records: Please review the health records for the pupils in your class. Check to see that any necessary referrals have been made and that all entries are complete and up to date.

1.3   PTA Events:
Evening meeting—Tuesday, November 20, 7:30 P.M.
Holiday Fair—Tuesday, December 4, Gym.
Holiday Show (Puppets)—Wednesday, December 12.
Kindergarten Show—Tuesday, December 18.

1.4   Traffic Safety: Please give lessons on proper crossing of streets. Stress the dangers of mid-block crossing, crossing where there is no guard, etc. In the lower grades, integrate this with your map and chart skills.

1.5   Science: You will soon receive a notice giving details of our Science Fair, which will take place the first week of February. Begin planning now for group and individual projects.

1.6   Literary Magazine: Please be sure that you are sending children's work to your grade leader on a regular basis. All teachers should be using the tally sheets distributed earlier this year.

II. Supervision and Improvement of Instruction.

2.1   Homework: Please review the circular distributed in September. Homework is never to be given as punishment. School policy is not to assign homework over weekends.

2.2   Bulletin Boards: Classroom bulletin boards are an effective way of vitalizing learning. Be sure that they are changed regularly to reflect *current* work. Also, make sure that all children have a chance sometime during the year to have at least one item displayed.

2.3   Math Activity Cards: Mrs. Bartone has prepared a series of 30 activity cards for intermediate grades in math. These self-directed cards provide fast-working pupils with some stimulating activity when they finish their classwork ahead of the others.

2.4   Questioning: An analysis of recent classroom observation reveals that many teachers can improve their techniques of questioning. We will discuss this at our grade level conferences. Be certain that you ask a balance of thought and fact questions.

2.5   Plan Books: In planning your week's work, give some attention to the teaching of skills in the area of physical education. Some teachers are merely providing their pupils with free play.

From the Principal's Desk

There is much to be gained when parents and teachers meet, face to face, to discuss the progress of pupils. You will have several opportunities to do this during the current school year. In addition to the afternoon Fall Conference on November 13 and the afternoon Spring Conference on April 13, a third date has been added: Tuesday afternoon, February 10.

We hope that all parents will take advantage of this opportunity. As in the past, one evening conference is planned for Tuesday evening, November 18. It is suggested that only those parents who can *not* come in the afternoon attend the evening conference. Parents of kindergarten and first-grade children will have a chance to confer with their children's teachers on Thursday, November 5 and Thursday, November 12. When you attend these sessions we hope that you will speak frankly to the teacher and listen attentively to the teacher's report on how your child acts in school. You should be interested in learning how another caring adult perceives your child.

American Education Week, commonly referred to as Open School Week, will be observed from November 17 through

November 21. At this time, you are invited to see your child's class in action. For many of you it will be a real eye-opener to observe the group dynamics that take place in a classroom. You will see how age peers of your child interact with one another and their teacher. Please do not bring pre-school age children with you. We want very much to avoid disturbing the usual classroom routines and deportment.

Please make full use of these opportunities to learn more about your child and his or her school life.

John Burrows
Principal

NOVEMBER CURRICULUM CALENDAR

1—Author's Day. Celebrated since 1928 on this date. Help pupils understand the creative process. Have them discuss some of their favorite authors.

(First Tuesday)—Election Day. Help pupils understand whom their parents are voting for. Discuss various offices. Write names of major candidates on the board. Do not pry into family confidences or give your own choice. Do urge the children to encourage their parents to vote.

11—Veterans' Day. Invite a veterans' organization to send a speaker to your school. Have intermediate grade pupils look up the history of the Tomb of the Unknown Soldier. Have older children discuss the concepts of war and peace.

19—Gettysburg Address. President Lincoln delivered his famous speech on this day. Have an articulate upper grade pupil commemorate the event by reading the address over the school's loudspeaker system.

(Fourth Thursday)—Thanksgiving Day. Have pupils draw pictures of those things for which they are most grateful.

Chapter 4

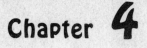

SUN	MON	TUES	WED	THU	FRI	SAT

DECEMBER

Organizing for a winter festival

One way to lift your school out of the midwinter doldrums is to organize a winter festival in which pupils and teachers can invite parents to "come look us over" in a positive, wholesome way. Here's how one junior high school goes about planning such an activity.

1. Tentative plans are made in November. A theme is selected by a committee of teachers and supervisors and presented to the entire staff for discussion and approval. A tentative date in December is set.

2. Department heads meet with all teachers in their areas to determine what department-wide presentations will be made, i.e., "The Wonderful World of Math" or "English as a Second Language." At this time, teachers may indicate preliminary plans for work to be shown by and from their own classes. By this time there has been preliminary planning with the students.

3. If the date selected is early January, teachers are asked to indicate what their classes will be presenting by December 1. No one, whether pupil or teacher, is required to participate.

4. A committee of teachers and one supervisor start preparation of tickets, programs, and other overall duplicated material, much of which is mimeographed by student teams

working with a paraprofessional. Other material is printed by the Graphic Arts squad, with their shop teacher.

5. The art department, in addition to preparing their own show of pupil art and/or special slides, photos, movies, and other visuals, prepares decorations for the corridors and bulletin boards and display cases that will not be preempted by other departments.

6. Coordination is done primarily by the department heads as a committee of the whole, assisted by a group of key teachers.

7. The supply committee, consisting of the teacher in charge of the supply room and the aides who work with him, lays in a supply of materials expected to be in greatest demand: masking tape, wrapping paper, markers, etc. The audio-visual squad and teacher coordinator get all equipment into shape: movie projectors, film strip and overhead and opaque projectors, various lamps and spare parts, radios, tape and disc recorders and players and, most recently, the video tape recorder and players.

8. The custodial staff is alerted and the custodian prepares to assist with extension cords, special furniture movement, and night duty.

9. School aides assist wherever needed, including typing, extra patrols, revised hours.

10. During midyear exam week in January, another meeting over lunch is held (dessert provided by the principal) to discuss further plans and overall problems.

11. Throughout, the union chapter chairman is made a part of the planning committee.

12. About a week before the Festival, teachers are asked to indicate space needs, whether in the lunchroom or in classrooms; the program committee is alerted and makes any room changes with classes where needed. Usually we use only the main floor.

13. On the day of the Festival, most classes are deeply involved in final preparations and rehearsals for the evening. We ignore class attendance on this day. We all do extra hall patrols so that all corridors are supervised as literally hundreds of students move about the building carrying materials and supplies from room to room. Teachers meet their classes in scheduled rooms, and, except for the chorus, band, and orchestra, students report in and then go on to assist with whatever projects they are working on.

14. The lunchroom manager is alerted earlier in the week and lunch is moved up to "brunch" so that the lunchroom may be cleared early in the day. Tables are washed down and those not needed for the evening Festival are removed.

15. The security squad and committee, having planned for admitting the more than 1,000 guests who generally attend, have arranged for school aides and monitors to be on duty for the evening, protecting equipment, helping supervise students, and assisting guests.

16. The hospitality committee has arranged for guides and posters advising guests of the location of restrooms and refreshment areas.

17. A faculty committee may want to arrange a teacher art or hobby show in one part of the building. This would not take away from the pupil efforts and would add another dimension to the Winter Festival.

18. Sufficient advance notice of the Festival is provided by the publicity committee as soon as the date and theme are set. Tickets are distributed on written request from parents and committee members. There is no charge, but the issuing of tickets prevents overcrowding and adds some status to the event.

19. Print the tickets in two different colors so that the big shows in the gym and in the auditorium can have guests channeled alternately.

20. Extend the mileage of this event by inviting the feeding elementary schools to come and visit your school during the next week. Those displays that do not interfere with lunch or other large activities can be left up for them to see.

Making the most of your guidance counselor

Are you getting the most service for pupils with adjustment or developmental problems? The clinical personnel such as psychologists, psychiatrists, and social workers are very expensive and difficult to obtain. During this holiday period many families are under stress and this certainly has an effect on their children. This is a good time to assess just how you are utilizing the services of your guidance counselor.

Generally speaking, he or she should be helping pupils, their teachers, and their parents in the following suggested manner:

The Counselor Assists Pupils:

Recommends special placement.
Conducts individual and small-group counseling.
Develops programs in career education.
Screens records.
Makes referrals for remedial instruction.
Suggests recreational facilities—camping, scouting, YMCA.
Makes referrals to mental hygiene or family service agencies.
Eases transitions between educational levels.
Orients new pupils.

The Counselor Assists Teachers:

Observes children referred by staff.
Conducts conferences on specific children's needs.
Shares information gleaned on children.
Conducts in-service courses and workshops.
Holds team and case conferences.
Demonstrates guidance techniques suitable for classroom teachers.
Sets up a guidance library including visual aids.
Conducts joint interviews with parents and teachers.

The Counselor Assists Parents:

Interviews parents who request counseling help.
Provides information about children's achievement.
Conducts workshops and study groups.
Acts as a resource person at PTA meetings and in community activities.
Interprets the school program.
Writes for PTA newsletter about child development.

A recent article in the *Wall Street Journal* emphasized the effect of federal funding on the growth of elementary school counseling on a national basis. Unlike high school guidance counselors, who spend most of their time helping adolescents who are in trouble and advising on job opportunities and college entrance requirements, elementary counselors aim at influencing youngsters before their problems get out of hand. A 1975 study at the University of North Dakota showed that a group of 34 pre-school children with whom a counselor worked thrice weekly for 11 weeks developed a better "self-concept." This was measured by improvement in 14 out of 25 categories, such as their willingness to share and their ability to work independently. A control group of 18 youngsters who didn't get counseling showed improvement in only one category. Take some time this month to analyze the guidance services you are getting and see how they can be improved.

Tips on improving pupil attendance

A school can provide a number of school attendance services without an organized program. But, like anything else, your effectiveness in raising the percent of attendance will increase as a result of coordinated attendance activities.

An organized attendance program reduces duplication, thus making it possible to extend services to more children. Also, an organized program makes it possible to anticipate the most critical needs. Many of these needs manifest themselves during the month of December.

The following organizational guidelines may be appropriate for development or modification of a program in all schools:

1. Prepare a clear-cut statement of the objectives of the program of in-school attendance services. These objectives should take into account the characteristics and the needs of the student body.

2. Determine precisely the functions of the school attendance program—that is, what the program should do for the students.

3. Assign specific duties to those who are to participate in the program. Allocate tasks to individuals on the basis of their qualifications for and their interest in the work; give them definite responsibilities for performing these tasks.

4. Give each person assigned to a task in school attendance authority commensurate with his ability.

5. Define clearly the working relationships.

6. Keep the plan or organization and its operations as simple as possible.

To be more specific in organizing the program, follow these suggestions:

1. Orient the pupils as to your expectations regarding uninterrupted and sequential instruction.
2. Involve the parents in a spirit of cooperation. Point out their responsibilities.
3. Hold faculty conferences devoted to creative approaches in fostering good attendance.
4. Give technical assistance to teachers in maintaining an accurate roll book and other school attendance procedures.
5. Provide for the mailing of postcards to the parents of absent pupils.
6. Utilize the school telephone to communicate with parents of school absentees.
7. Insist on a note from parents for all absences.
8. Schedule interviews with parents of children who do not come to school on an individual basis.
9. Involve the school doctor and nurse in conferences on school attendance.
10. Refer chronic and long-term absentees to the attendance teacher for home visits.
11. Establish incentive awards, assembly programs, bulletin boards, posters and end-of-term awards in recognition of good school attendance.
12. Prepare a pupil-devised handbook to include expectations regarding punctuality and school attendance.

Your approach to suspending pupils

There comes a time when for the health and safety of other children or even for his or her own safety you must suspend a pupil. These disciplinary exclusions are usually very infrequent. Sometimes they are resorted to only after other means have been tried, such as sending home to "cool off," placing in special classes, or transferring among schools or districts. The leading cause, according to a study by the Children's Defense Fund (CDF), was "fighting"—36.6%. CDF also found that there is a great variation in the length of suspensions and in the number and kinds of offenses. Statistically a child is more likely to be suspended if he is black, poor and in high school. Few districts have clear, written and consistent rules of conduct, the study contends. As a result, the actions that can lead to suspension are defined by individual administrators.

We suggest that instead of suspension you try some alternatives, such as behavior contracts, student ombudsmen, peer group counseling, and in-school centers. This is not to say that when all else has failed you must not be able to rid the classroom of disruptive pupils who divert the teacher's attention from others.

Figure 4-1 presents suggested suspension notice.

Dear_____:

I regret to inform you that it has become necessary to suspend your daughter/son_____

　　　　　　　　　(Full name—last name may differ from parent)

of Class_____for a period of four (4) days, beginning_____19____ for_____

_____
　　　　　　　　(Give specific incident succinctly.)

A conference is scheduled for_____at_____o'clock. At that time you will have an opportunity to examine and discuss the relevant facts with all the parties concerned so that we may plan together for_____'s return to school.

During the period of suspension,_____should be kept home during school hours.

　　　　　　　　　　　　　　　　　　　　Yours truly,

FIGURE 4-1

After you have conducted the suspense hearing it is very valuable to keep a summary of what took place (Figure 4-2). You may want to duplicate several copies of this form so that you can forward one to the district office and keep one in the pupil's folder and one in your file.

Making the most of school clubs

A more positive approach to channeling the energies of pupils is to provide opportunities within the school day for special interest activities or clubs.

As it gets more and more expensive to keep school buildings open on weekends or after the regular closing hours, principals have turned to a club hour or workshop hour during the school

SUMMARY OF PRINCIPAL'S SUSPENSE HEARING

Name of pupil_____ Date of pre-suspense
                                     letter sent_____

Address_____ Date of pre-suspense
_____   conference_____

Date of birth_____ Date of principal's
                                     suspense conference

Telephone_____ _____

Class_____ Teacher_____

Date pupil entered school   Date of return to school
_____   _____

Current attendance for this school year:
Present_____Absent_____Late_____Cuts_____
Agency, if any, to which pupil is known:
Name of worker on case:
Result of Agency contact:
Persons present at Conference:

Reason(s) (specific) for suspension:

Efforts of school personnel prior to suspension:

Action(s) to be taken as a result of hearing:
1. By school personnel

2. By pupil

3. By parent(s) of pupil

Any other comments:

FIGURE 4-2

week. They have also found that this stimulates good school attendance. By including teachers in the initial planning you will get their support and encouragement.

In order to give you a specific plan for setting up such a program within an elementary school, we are providing you with a set of instructions just as they were handed out to the staff of an elementary school *after* the principal had worked out the general guidelines with the teachers.

Ladies and Gentlemen:

Beginning on Tuesday, January 16, the last hour of each Tuesday, Wednesday, and Thursday from 1:30 to 2:30 P.M. will be designated as the "Club Hour" for Grades 4 and 5. This is to afford our children who are on grade and better in their fundamentals an opportunity to explore curriculum areas of their own choosing for greater self-expression. Those children who are below grade in fundamentals will be programmed by their teachers for remedial groups in reading and arithmetic. Certain groups will be pre-programmed by the classroom teacher (band, reading, mathematics).

The offerings this year will be as follows:

GROUP	TEACHER	ROOM
Senior Band	Mr. Del Rio	101
Junior Band	Miss Roose	105
Reading Improvement	Mrs. Morse	201
Math Skills	Mrs. Levin	207
Dramatics	Mr. Bonde	Aud.
Creative Writing	Miss Cheek	203
Art and Ceramics	Mrs. Ford	214
Ballet	Miss Smith	112
Italian Language and Culture	Mrs. Discenza	208
Photography	Mr. De Leon	210
Woodworking	Mrs. Merman	118
Sports Skills	Mr. Carling	Gym

This program is frankly experimental in its attempt to fulfill the special needs of each child. Its success will depend on the cooperation of staff in assigning children properly and on the ability to keep groups at a 30 maximum (equalize where necessary).

Teachers of these specialty groups should have a plan for the term (about 15 weeks) worked out, with time blocks for various activities included. It is the responsibility of each teacher to obtain special materials for each group (except remedial reading and math) but, where possible, G. O. funds will be drawn upon for reasonable purchases and aid is usually proffered by our P.T.A. when specific needs are shown. The accompanying form should be used by each child to "register" for his group. Music and remedial children must be identified by the classroom teacher, and these children are to be told to fill in their forms with these "choices." Also, please screen applicants for the Creative Writing group to be sure they qualify by virtue of special talent and interest. Explain to children that some may need to accept a second choice or a third choice to equalize groups and that some may have to accept a compromise choice. This year, because of early bus schedules, workshops will run from 1:30 to 2:30 P.M. Please feel free to see me about any phase of this plan not covered in this memo.

Yours truly,

As a follow-up, the form shown in Figure 4-3 was sent home to parents by their children.

PUPIL REGISTRATION FORM FOR CLUB HOUR GROUP
GRADES 4 and 5

Please check first, second, and third choices of groups offered below.

Band and remedial groups have been pre-selected; pupils must designate these as their first choice if they have been selected for these groups.

CHOICE			CLUB	ROOM
First	*Second*	*Third*		
—	—	—	Senior Band	101
—	—	—	Junior Band	105
			Remedial Reading	201
			Remedial Math	207
			Dramatics	Aud.
			Creative Writing	203
			Art and Ceramics	214
			Ballet	112
			Italian Lang. & Culture	208
			Photography	210
			Woodworking	118
			Sports Skills	Gym

Pupil's Name_____ Class_____ Parent's Initials____ Date____

FIGURE 4-3

By involving the teachers from the start you can be more certain of their interest and support. It is also important to discuss these plans with the leadership of the P.T.A. to insure their financial backing and thorough understanding of how well this instructional time is being spent. This will blunt the thrust of some minority complaints about the use of valuable school time for frills. Encourage teachers to relate the learnings of the regular school program to the club hour.

Involving the community in school zoning

Periodically, school boundaries and zones have to be redrawn. This is done for a variety of reasons: construction of new housing developments, opening of new schools, improving integration. District Office staffs and school principals have a responsibility to make everyone in the community aware of the proposed plan. Do not wait until the last line is drawn and then announce it as a *fait accompli.*

Local businessmen, realtors, bankers, and transportation companies as well as parents and teachers have a stake in school zone changes. A series of open meetings, held at convenient hours, should be set up. Speakers at earlier meetings should be invited by letter, as should those citizens who have written to make suggestions. The following memorandum illustrates these ideas clearly.

FERNWOOD SCHOOL BOARD
MEMORANDUM

To: Members, Community School Board #3
Dr. Ellis Woodbury, Superintendent
Principals, Fernwood Schools
Fernwood Teachers' Association
Presidents, Parents' Associations
Mayor's Office
Federation of Community Organizations
Central Student Council
Speakers at first public meeting, November 12
Writers of correspondence on zoning
FROM: Frank Reynolds, Assistant Superintendent for High Schools

RE: FERNWOOD HIGH SCHOOL ZONING

The second public meeting in this year's annual review of the re-zoning plan has been scheduled as follows:

Tuesday, December 16   Susan **B.** Anthony HS Auditorium
     3:00 to 5:00 P.M.   and 7:00 to 9:00 **P.M.**

The first half hour of each session will be used to explain the tentative proposal. A copy of this proposal was mailed early in November. This proposal was developed within the guidelines of the objectives discussed at the first meeting, after a careful study of the diverse input from the above groups.

I invite you to share with us your concerns and comments on the proposal. Additional copies will be available at the meeting. If you would like us to give you an additional copy before the meeting, please stop by the District Office. Since the purpose of this meeting is to hear and record your ideas and feelings, you will be able to arrange for speaking time when you arrive. You need not, therefore, make prior arrangements for speaking time.

If you are able to join us and if you have not already done so you may send us your written suggestions before December 16. Please write "Fernwood Zoning" on your envelope to expedite its handling and study. We will then prepare a proposed plan, reflecting all input, which will be presented to Supt. Woodbury. His zoning plan will be issued as soon as possible thereafter.

FRANK REYNOLDS
Assistant Superintendent
for High Schools

Focusing on teachers' lessons

The most important role the principal faces is that of im-prover of instruction. While good school managers are sure to get around their buildings frequently, these classroom visits tend to be cursory. You should make it a practice to conduct formal, scheduled observations of lessons at least once each year for every teacher you supervise.

Once you have established that policy you will find it easy to put into practice if you mimeograph letters similar to the one in Figure 4-4 that you and your department heads can send to teachers each year:

Date

Dear_____:

I am planning to observe you teach a lesson of approximately 30 minutes in the area of_____. Please indicate below which of these two dates is more convenient. Also indicate the time you would like me to come into your room.

Please hand in a Lesson Plan a day earlier. Include Aim, Motivation, Procedures, etc. Indicate also past and future learnings touching this lesson.

After this lesson we will hold a post-observation conference during your preparation period. If you would like to meet me prior to your lesson, please let me know.

Sincerely,

DATES:_____197___
_____197___

My preference is_____ at_____ AM/PM

FIGURE 4-4

Gaining good will through food sharing

Breaking bread together has for centuries been a symbol of peace and good will. It certainly works in school situations when parents and teachers or parents and parents gather around a food table buffet, coffee urn, or snack bar to share ideas and food.

Perhaps your school has pupils coming from many different ethnic backgrounds. You can reduce tensions, teach respect for diversity of peoples, and have genuine fun at an International Luncheon. Plan ahead of time to have parents prepare a national or regional dish that can easily be served in school. Have the pupils write a short description of the dish and where it comes from. After the initial planning, the pupils can make a spirit master cookbook to be distributed at the luncheon. The commonality of certain favorite ingredients and the contributions of various cultures to our tastes will help to reduce differences and enhance respect for all peoples. Some schools have encouraged pupils to wear the clothing that is usually associated with the regions where the food originated.

You can also use ethnic foods to teach a variety of subjects, as did an intermediate school in Jackson Heights, N.Y. They were able to use family foods and receipes to increase an understanding of the social sciences by talking about regions and locating them on maps. Attention was paid to products of different lands and their folklore as it involves food. Math students calculated calories for such dishes as Slavic pita (Near Eastern bread) and Icelandic pancakes. A single dish, arroz con pollo (chicken and rice casserole), brought forth many different recipes from different parts of the Spanish-speaking world. The art class made posters and the graphic arts class printed a mimeographed cookbook containing the various recipes and pupil names.

By sharing their recipes, the different ethnic groups were able to see the common thread that tasty dishes weave through our culture. They also saw how a single dish can have different names in different countries. By breaking bread together the children and their parents were able to put aside differences and emphasize their common likes

Christmas is an excellent time of year to focus on different kinds of celebrations. Have pupils prepare multi-lingual greeting cards or share different types of tree ornaments.

Preparing for a winter recess room clean-up

Everyone looks forward to the Christmas vacation. For the custodial staff of your school the days between Christmas Day and New Year's Day are spent cleaning the building and doing those small paint jobs and other clean-up details that they can't do during the school year. You can help your custodian do a better job by getting your teachers to cooperate.

Distribute a letter like the one in Figure 4-5 to your teachers with space for them to check off each item as they do it. This will help everyone come back to a cleaner school. You might include a reminder about room keys, which should be stored in a safe place. Occasionally vandals will break into a school during the holiday season and if the room doors are unlocked or if the room keys are easily accessible, much more damage can be done more quickly.

```
┌─────────────────────────────────────────────────────────────┐
│                  WINTER RECESS ROOM CLEAN-UP                 │
│ Teachers:                                                    │
│    During the winter recess your room will be cleaned by the │
│ custodial staff. Please help by seeing to it that the following items │
│ are taken care of.                                           │
│ __  1. Begin to dispose of unwanted papers and materials today. Do │
│         not wait until the day before the holiday.           │
│ __  2. Clear off all cabinet tops.                           │
│ __  3. Store all materials in closets. Remove jars of paint and put │
│         easels in wardrobes.                                 │
│ __  4. Leave nothing (brief cases, book bags, sneakers, etc.) on the │
│         floor of the room or coat closet.                    │
│ __  5. Have pupils empty their desks. Pupils' books may be stored │
│         in closets or taken home on a staggered basis.       │
│ __  6. Clear off window sills. Send home plants.             │
│ __  7. Remove decorations from doors and windows.            │
│ __  8. Clean out chalk troughs. Have pupils wash boards.     │
│ __  9. Be sure that children take home pets and fish.        │
│ __ 10. If you are having a class party do NOT have it on the last day │
│         of school. Have it on the day before instead.        │
│            HAVE A HAPPY AND ENJOYABLE HOLIDAY!               │
└─────────────────────────────────────────────────────────────┘
```

FIGURE 4-5

Planning a Bill of Rights Week

In many states a Bill of Rights Week is celebrated during the week of December 15, which is National Bill of Rights Day. To make such a week more meaningful, schools are encouraged to relate the provisions of the Declaration of Independence and other important documents to recent occurrences in schools and in society at large.

Students may find it interesting to compare the list of grievances against the king contained in the Declaration of Independence with the content of the first ten amendments, which comprise the Federal Bill of Rights. They might examine the Bill of Rights in the State Constitution, if there is one, to learn that resistance to tyranny against persons has been of importance at this level also.

Since the initial development of the Bill of Rights, many people have profited from these guarantees, largely as a result of court interpretation of these provisions. An examination of a Supreme Court decision such as *in re Gault* (1967) would give students an understanding of the real meaning of the Court's extension of these rights, since the case involved a teen-aged boy, accused of wrongdoing, who had been deprived of his civil rights by lower courts.

When you get a few minutes to reflect ask yourself these questions: Do your social studies activities give all students the opportunity to feel a part of the activity? Does the school program recognize what this country has become, rather than simply what it once was?

Does the school provide a curriculum that focuses upon the rule of law? A law-related curriculum gives students the opportunity to look at both the nation's history and its future, in terms of extension of rights and of needs for greater guarantees in the future. Are your students playing an active role in the learning processes? Do they learn to analyze situations rather than to memorize the results of someone else's analysis? Are they given opportunity to develop and improve decision-making skills?

Spend some time in pupil assemblies talking to your pupils about the rule of law. Set up a school court or other tribunal to which pupils can come to get a fair shake in disciplinary cases. Encourage legal professionals (district attorneys, lawyers, legal aid people) to come and talk to classes and groups.

Go to your district office and find out how your school can qualify for a grant under the National Endowment for the Humanities to provide law-related education for your school. Monies have been available for the training of teachers and administrators.

Sample conference notes

STAFF CONFERENCE

December 17, 19____

A long dispute means that both parties are wrong.

—Voltaire

I.   Acknowledgments.

    1.1   Thanks and appreciation for:

        The excellent job being done by our Parent Reading Volunteers.

        The hard work and thoughtfulness of our PTA as shown in our recent Holiday Fair and Christmas Show.

        The fine showing made by Hutchinson pupils in contributing toys for the needy.

        The continued good tone and appearance of our school, thanks to your efforts.

II.   Administrative Notes.

    1.1   Attendance Periods: The fourth attendance period ends December 21. Total days this period—15. Total days to date—68.

    1.2   Pupil Attendance: Average percentage of attendance in November was 94%, ninth highest in the county. The attendance officer tells us that a Form 47 is to be sent out when a child has been absent because of illness for more than ten days, not necessarily consecutively. A home visit will be made.

    1.3   Borrowed Items: In order not to inconvenience your fellow teachers, please return all borrowed items (TV sets, audio-visual supplies, math lab materials) before the holiday recess.

    1.4   Fire Drills: The last two fire drills were considerably better than the two held before them. Please praise your classes for this improvement.

    1.5   Literary Magazine: Please continue to send work to your grade leaders regularly.

    1.6   Social Studies: Discussion of the course of study. Leaders: Mrs. Rolo and Mrs. Baer.

Next conference: Monday, January 21.

SINCERE BEST WISHES FOR A HAPPY HOLIDAY

From the Principal's Desk

Dear Parents:

In keeping with our efforts to do the utmost for all of the children I once again ask for your cooperation and assistance in the matter of pupil attendance.

I have stressed many times the importance of regular attendance in order that each child receive the maximum benefits from regular daily sequential instruction.

We urge all our parents to assist us in our goals, which we all realize are necessary to give our children every opportunity to benefit from regular attendance at school.

Of course, children cannot attend when they are ill, but there are few—very few—other reasons for non-attendance. However, it is better for a child to come to school late or for part of the day than to miss the entire day.

I know I have the cooperation of all of our parents.

Sincerely,

Sam Nicholas
Principal

DECEMBER CURRICULUM CALENDAR

5—Phillis Wheatley died in 1884. This black woman was a famous poet during the colonial period. Some of her poems are suitable for reading aloud on almost any grade level.

6—St. Nicholas Day. Research this holiday as it is enjoyed in Belgium. Have your pupils contrast the appearance of St. Nicholas, Kris Kringle, Father Christmas, and, of course, Santa Claus.

8-Day Period in December (consult Jewish calendar). Hanukkah, the Festival of Lights. The candles on the Hanukkah menorah will burn in many Jewish homes during this week of December. Show the McGraw-Hill filmstrip "Hanukkah." Or ask the librarian for some Jewish holiday books.

7—Pearl Harbor Day. Anniversary of Japan's surprise attack in 1941. Locate Pearl Harbor on a wall map. Discuss current relations with Japan.

16—Boston Tea Party. In 1773 there was a raid on three British ships by American patriots. Discuss importance of tea in colonial times.

21—Pilgrims land at Plymouth Rock, 1620. Set up committees to study the contributions of immigrants to this country. Consider why each group left their homeland to come to this shore. Start with the Pilgrims.

Chapter 5

SUN	MON	TUES	WED	THU	FRI	SAT
		JANUARY				

Making the most of bilingual opportunities

Most school administrators agree that a much greater awareness, understanding and appreciation of our pluralistic society is needed. One step towards the ultimate goal of having a multicultural instructional program in all schools is to set up a bilingual/bicultural instructional program where you have a large percent of the pupil population representing a single ethnic group. In many of our schools there is an American Indian, Chicano, Puerto Rican, Italian, Haitian, or other minority group that represents a large block of pupils.

In Denver, the new Del Pueblo Elementary School is giving the community a greater understanding of the many contributions Hispanic people have made to the development of our nation. A team of graduate students from the University of Colorado School of Social Work made a survey of parents and found that 96% of them felt that it was important that their children learn the value of the Spanish language and their own cultural heritage. As one parent commented: "All we know is the American society. Our culture is beautiful and is nothing to be ashamed of."

Throughout the school this goal is being realized. It is always combined with equal concern for the program's current goals: the development of a pupil's English language proficiency and awareness of United States history and culture.

The Del Pueblo Elementary School is a school of 450 pupils, divided by age into five "families." The four oldest are known by Mexican Indian names. The six- and seven-year olds are Toltecs; the next eldest are Zapotecs; next come the Mayans; and finally the ten- and eleven-year olds, Aztecs. The Hijitos are the pre-school or four- and five-year olds.

One teacher serves as a resource teacher and implements the program. She develops monthly cultural activities and guides. She also sets up Spanish language units that teachers can use to incorporate Spanish language and culture into the regular curriculum. With the help of other bilingual teachers and paraprofessionals, the resource teacher also gives several one-half hour weekly Spanish language lessons to each family and conducts special classes for monolingual students and those with advanced Spanish skills.

Following the formal Spanish lesson, the classroom teacher conducts practice lessons, reinforcing material covered by the resource teacher. "We're all learning Spanish together, and we speak more and more in class and to each other," comments a teacher in the Aztec family. "In September the kids wouldn't admit to speaking Spanish," she adds. "Now they love it."

Many of the families have been in the United States for three or more generations. While most of the students have Spanish surnames, only about one-fifth are Spanish speaking.

For additional language experience students watch "Villa Alegre," a combined Spanish/English public television show for kids. Activities are planned to help students develop a greater awareness of and pride in Mexican Indian and Southwestern United States culture. This is done through studies in history, culture, fine arts and folk art, and also by using as many cultural resources as possible. For example, a group of Mexican cowboys demonstrated their skill in handling a rope in the assembly. A bulletin board features "Amigos"—photos of Spanish-surnamed neighborhood people who serve as community helpers.

Many of these instructional units expand the bicultural approach to a more multicultural one, reinforcing the idea that diversity is to be enjoyed by all Americans.

Developing a concern for safety

At faculty conferences and when meeting with small groups of teachers, remind them of their need to be alert in the area of pupil safety. This 18- point checklist will help you be specific:

1. Study all emergency drill regulations and see that official cards are posted in classrooms.
2. Inspect furniture in classrooms to see that tables and chairs are solidly placed.
3. Remove those articles that may fall from tops of cabinets or shelves and cause an injury.
4. Do not put objects on outside window sills.
5. Place window pole securely in the receptacle provided.
6. Supervise the change of classes and dismissal according to school routines.
7. Do not ask children to move heavy objects. Use caution and good judgment.
8. Do not allow pupils to handle any electrical equipment without direct supervision of the teacher. Teach how to do this safely. (Warn against pulling plug from wall by yanking wire.)
9. Inspect all machines operated by electric current for defective wiring (AV equipment).
10. Teach children to open and close doors slowly, and to look back before closing or letting go of door.
11. Plan for good arrangement of chairs in order to facilitate normal, safe classroom traffic.
12. Teach care in proper use of sharp, pointed objects.
13. Caution children against placing objects in their mouths.
14. Prohibit the use of improvised ladders such as wobbly chairs or boxes placed on chairs or desks.
15. Teach good housekeeping in the classroom.
16. Caution children to keep feet well under the desk or table to avoid tripping others.
17. Caution children about dangers involved in handling glass objects.
18. Notify the principal when a child reports to school with an arm or leg in a cast.

We also have a responsibility to teach safety in the home. Here is a list, in order of importance, of the ten accident hazards reported most frequently by children. Use this list as a basis for safety lessons.

1. Is there a sturdy wall "grabber" to help one get out of the tub or shower?
2. Have you a first aid booklet to tell you what to do in case of accidents?
3. Do all members of the family wear slippers or shoes to protect their feet when walking around the house?
4. Do you have pads or non-slip backing under all small rugs and mats?
5. Do you avoid having more than one lamp or appliance attached to a wall outlet at a time?

Encourage your teachers to have their pupils enter a traffic safety poster contest. Provide them with a theme and some simple rules to follow. Your PTA or local service club will be glad to furnish prizes for the best posters if you include them as judges.

Suggested theme: "Help Your Safety Patrol"
Suggested rules:

1. Designs must be on tag board or poster paper. The overall size should be 15" x 20" or 14" x 22" with a 3" space left at the bottom.
2. Lettering must be clearly legible. Do not use stenciled or traced letters.
3. There is no limitation on the type of media—paint, crayon, felt pen, cut paper, etc.
4. Illustrations should be positive in approach, showing only correct traffic behavior (cars always on the proper side of the street, for instance).
5. Include on the back of the poster:

       Pupil's name:
       Home address:
       Phone:
       Age:
       School and class:

Tips for involving the community

Among the greatest community resources available are the grandparents of your school's pupils. The parents may both work or be involved in many activities while the grandparents are available and eager to help young people. Who can provide love and affection better than the experts—grandma and grandpa? In Columbus, Ohio a Grandparent Program has been in operation in the elementary schools. The teachers plan a very flexible schedule for the grandparents. Even though they are scheduled on a specific day, the "experts" are invited to drop in at any time. After all, love and affection work as well on a moment's notice as they do in scheduled doses. Grandparents in that city enjoy sharing children's successes, listening to them read, playing games with them, reading stories to them, showing appreciation for their talents and achievements, giving them hugs and kisses, and doing "other things that grandparents do best."

The interaction between school and community is a two-way street. The school needs to consider the needs and resources of other community agencies. Frequently the local public library gets annoyed with the school that sends hordes of pupils down to look for the same book or to research the same topic at the same time. The Northbrook, Illinois schools have eliminated this vexation by printing postcards called "Assignment Alert Card" and distributing them to all teachers. It ensures that pupils will have a successful experience at the library, which in turn warms them up to using the library and doing research.

The message side of the card looks something like Figure 5-1.

You can vitalize the history curriculum of your school by having pupils talk to people who remember the events being studied. In contrast to the traditionally political orientation of high school history classes, you can encourage pupils to see history as it relates to people. How did the lives of people of other eras respond to the demands of their physical environment and culture?

Some Missouri high school students helped formulate a course titled "Adventure in American Social and Cultural History." It was supported by a grant from the National Endowment for the Humanities. Working from first-person accounts and information gained from existing records and memorabilia,

---

ASSIGNMENT ALERT CARD

Dear Librarian:

I have given my students the following library research assignment:

Could you please have appropriate materials on hand and accessible—specifically including the following:

Thank you.

                    _____
                    (Teacher's Name)
                    Grade or Class_____
                    School_____

FIGURE 5-1

each student constructed his own local history. The interviews, most of which were conducted in the homes of the older generation, were recorded on more than 30 hours of tape. Many artifacts— quilts, baskets, churns, etc.—became an important part of the interview. The students uncovered a gold mine of documents, photographs, correspondence and newspapers. Students spent many months learning how to treat old documents so they could be handled without damage, and they divided into groups to catalog the findings and write articles on family life, schools, churchs, race relations, government and business. These were compiled in booklet form and sales in the community helped pay for printing costs.

These suggestions will help you build bridges of understanding and support between your school and the larger community.

Your responsibility in cases of child abuse

There is increasing evidence emerging each day of child abuse and maltreatment at home. Almost all states have passed some kind of child protective services act. These mandate the reporting by school authorities of all cases of child abuse and maltreatment. Administrators who willfully fail to do so are guilty of a misdemeanor.

Time spent at a faculty conference discussing aspects of protective laws, especially by a knowledgeable guest speaker, will be well spent. An important responsibility that you have as head of the school is to make certain that your teachers know how to report such cases correctly. These nine points are musts in any oral or written report your school makes:

1. The names and addresses of the child and the parents or other persons responsible for his or her care, if known.
2. The child's age, sex, and race (unless prohibited by law).
3. The nature and extent of the child's injuries, abuse or maltreatment including any evidence of prior injuries, abuse or maltreatment to the child or his siblings.
4. The names of the person or persons responsible for causing the injury, abuse or maltreatment, if known.
5. Family composition.
6. The source of the report.
7. The person making the report and where he or she can be reached.
8. The actions taken by the reporting source, including the taking of photographs and x-rays, removal or keeping of the child or notifying the medical examiner.
9. Any other information which the Commissioner or other municipal or state protective officer may require. Or any other facts that the person making the report thinks may be helpful.

You will be on the horns of a dilemma about reporting some cases of neglect or abuse. Just remember that if you keep the welfare of the child in mind, no one can fault you for taking the wrong course. In some cases, the best thing may be to overlook some isolated instances. On other occasions it may be best for you to report the matter to the appropriate authority. In recent years the number of cases reported has increased significantly. Many experts feel that this is due not entirely to a more sadistic society, but in large measure to more frequent reporting by school authorities. Be sure that your staff is aware of the chain of referral in these cases. You must be told before any outside agency gets a report. Nothing could be more embarrassing than having a teacher report such a case without your knowing about it.

How to spark the in-service training of teachers

In-service programs are changing, based in part on successful practices by industry and in part on teacher demands to take an active role in developing training programs that have a significant impact on their future. In the past, in-service courses were often conducted behind the ivied walls of a university by college professors who hadn't been near a public school in years. Now most school districts are carrying the ball themselves and many have a separate office of staff development.

January is a good time to plan your spring in-service courses and workshops. The spring term is less frantic for teachers and they are ready for some new ideas. In recent years there has been such chaos in September, with budget cuts and other last-minute changes in personnel, that administrators have not been able to offer meaningful courses until the spring semester.

In some places the school district and the teacher association or union are partners in developing in-service programs. Teachers are determining the content of programs through needs assessment, and they are planning and leading programs through their own skills. In other places, teachers are involved in administering and evaluating programs and in determining criteria for credit.

The whole matter of credit for coursework can create problems. One way to encourage master teachers to offer an in-service course when no money is available for payment is to award them the same number of credits as the teacher taking the course. Some course leaders require a great deal of outside work for completion of their program, while other courses require little if any extra work. It is important to try to standardize the credits and work requirements.

Teachers need an inducement to take in-service training, and many districts are taking their cue from industry, recognizing that it is in their own best interest to provide time, money and support for staff development. Many districts provide local funds for in-service training and are looking to state and federal sources for additional money. Others reimburse teachers for tuition, and some hire substitutes to make in-service programs possible. School officials used to expect teachers to participate in in-service training after school or on weekends, but they now realize that productive change can best be brought about by providing for in-service training on "company time."

In some cases the courts are getting into the act by mandating staff development as an integral part of court-ordered school reform. In Philadelphia, for example, a judge mandated changes in staff development of Title I, ESEA teachers. And in Dallas, in-service education was expanded greatly after a unique court decree ordered the district to create an affirmative action staff development program to remedy institutional racial discrimination.

Ten ways to save fuel in your school

The heat is on the school administrator to come to grips with long-range forecasts of continued high fuel costs. No one wants to see children sit in cold classrooms with their coats on. There are several things you and your custodian can do to conserve fuel. Here are ten of them:

1. Maintain classrooms and offices at 68-70 degrees.
2. Operate indirect ventilating systems in areas such as gyms and auditoriums only when they are in use.
3. Replace broken window panes or back them up promptly.
4. Clean fire sides of boilers every 100 hours of operation.
5. Check combustion regularly for proper CO_2 percentage.
6. Report leaks on steam and condensate lines promptly.
7. Shut header valves controlling steam to sections of the building not in use for activities.
8. Keep door checks on exterior doors in good operating condition.
9. Turn off lights when not in use.
10. Check closely fuel oil temperatures to provide for proper combustion. The quality of oil delivered may change during the winter. A close check on combustion should be kept after the delivery of each new load of oil.

Getting an extra hour out of every day

This is a basic challenge for all of us. We've discussed this challenge with action- and results-oriented principals we knew. Together, we've come up with many practical ways to secure one more precious hour from each day. (Remember that each of these tips is probably adaptable to your specific situation if you try to analyze your habits. Recognize the fact that the way you are doing something now *might* not be the best way.) Here they are. We hope you'll find them helpful and useful.

- Make up and follow a detailed, daily schedule.
- Avoid people who you know will waste your time—even if they are pleasant and seem to like you.
- If you commute to work, use the time to study or plan. Save the newspaper for the return trip home.
- Organize your work; do it systematically. Imagine that some efficiency expert is following you around.
- Make creative use of lunchtime. Invite some teachers or pupils in for some brainstorming on a mutually vexing problem.
- Spend less time on the phone.
- Delegate more authority if possible.
- Think first; then do the job.
- Work hardest when you're mentally most alert. This will be midmorning for most.
- Always do the toughest jobs first.
- Before each major act, ask: Is this *really* necessary?
- Write notes or letters while waiting for others.
- Concentrate on the specific task you are performing. This will avoid your having to redo it.
- Always carry a pencil and paper to capture important-to-you ideas.
- Nap an hour after dinner. Then take a shower. Begin the evening hours relaxed and refreshed.
- Avoid making a production out of small tasks.

And there you have it—more than 60 minutes worth of extra time that can be yours every single school day. Many of these ideas can be adapted to help give you more time for the things you really want to do on weekends and holidays as well.

Examples of activities that improve attendance

If you want to improve the attendance of your teachers, the best way to do it is to praise those teachers who have good attendance. For example, around January 15 put up a list of names over the time clock or in some other prominent spot. Over the list of names, write the question: "What do these people have in common?" After a while people will realize that these are the names of the teachers who have not been absent all year. This will make the people with perfect attendance as well as the others think twice before they take a day off. Another good way is to always ask teachers how they are feeling when they return from a day off.

Have you noticed how two schools in the same district with similar pupil populations can have vastly different percentages of pupil attendance? We've talked to administrators in schools with the highest pupil attendance in their districts and have come up with this list of activities and procedures that you can adapt to your situation:

1. The principal speaks to parents at PTA meetings and also individually about the need for regular pupil attendance.
2. An advisory committee was set up consisting of teachers, parents and administrators with the goal of improving attendance.
3. If a child returned to school without an absence note, a form letter was sent home to the parent, requesting the reason for the absence.
4. Interviews with parents whose children had poor attendance were held with a view to removing obstacles to regular attendance.
5. Teachers engaged in an art program preparing banners for classes with 100% attendance.
6. It was suggested to teachers that if they expected to be absent the following day, they did NOT make this announcement to the pupils.
7. The principal spoke to the pupils during assemblies, in classrooms, and individually about the importance of regular attendance.
8. Each day one child from each class that had 100% attendance came to the office to personally announce the good news to the entire school over the loudspeaker.
9. Pupils with perfect attendance for the month were mentioned in the PTA newsletter.
10. Award assemblies were held every month for all classes where children with perfect attendance for that period received attendance buttons.
11. Where possible, a paraprofessional or school aide made phone calls to the homes of absent children. Postcards were sent if there was no telephone response.
12. The school nurse was involved in hard core absence cases.

How to arrange a "Nostalgia Night"

What's the best way to find out what life was like in the 1920's? How can you get old-timers to talk with teenagers? These are questions that faced a high school class in Delaware recently. They wanted more than the obvious sources of information, such as books published during that period. Instead, they arranged a Nostalgia Night in cooperation with the Newark, Delaware Senior Citizens Center. By doing this they entered a kind of time machine. The students visited the center and interviewed people who lived during that decade. This technique not only gave the young people new insights and new feelings for the Roaring 20s, it also gave the older people much pleasure to be cast in the role of experts. They liked being looked up to by young people.

The class was divided into six groups, and each group was given specific questions and general topics to explore:

- What were your feelings about prohibition?
- How were you personally affected by the '29 Stock Market crash?
- What plans for the future were you making as a teen-ager?
- What happened in your town the day it received news of Lindbergh's successful flight across the Atlantic?
- Was there really a feeling of prosperity in the 20's?
- Was the Teapot Dome scandal as involved as Watergate?
- How did the automobile affect your life in the 20's?
- What major differences do you see when you compare today with the 1920's?

Another kind of Nostalgia Night is when you invite into the school parents and other members of the community who graduated during a certain ten-year period. They recall old times in the school and the community. Young people love to hear stories of what took place when their parents were young.

Sample conference notes

STAFF CONFERENCE

January 20, 19___

I.   Reporting to Parents.

There will be parent-teacher conferences on Tuesday, February 11. Kindergarten classes will be scheduled for a shortened session on that day. All other classes will be dismissed at noon.

II. ZOOmobile.

Again this year the zoo will visit schools where teachers have prepared their pupils for such a visit. Each class participating in the program is expected to visit the zoo after the ZOOmobile has come to their class. Call Miss Stanton.

III. Student Teachers.

Our school is fortunate in being selected again this year to receive student teachers from the State University. Those teachers who requested student teachers in the fall term and did not get one will have a student teacher assigned next month.

IV. Guest Speaker.

Professor Peter Babcox of the State University. Topic: P.S. 5 as a Campus School.

V. Pupil Health.

It is part of each teacher's responsibility to record health data on each pupil's health card. This includes hearing and vision test results obtained by the nurse.

VI. Report Cards.

Marking period ends 1/31.
Report cards due in supervisor's office on 2/3.
Report cards distributed on 2/6.

VII. Classroom Doors.

In order to conserve heat and also to reduce noise, please keep your classroom doors closed. This is especially necessary if you are using a phonograph or other audio aid. Do not obstruct door windows completely—this is not a good safety practice.

From the Principal's Desk

Many slow starters win in the end! This is an observation that was made recently in a feature story in the *Chicago Daily News*. Its point was that parents should not despair if their schoolbound genius gets off to a shaky start on his or her road to fame. It cites a British pediatrician who has checked the childhood histories of persons destined for world acclaim and found that many were not considered bright youngsters.

Thomas Edison was consistently at the bottom of his class and his teacher said his mind was "addled."

Albert Einstein was unsociable and mentally slow. James Watt was "dull and inept."

Paul Gaugin was a dreamer who was "completely indifferent to lessons." Auguste Rodin was described as the "worst pupil in school." His father said, "I have an idiot for a son."

Many geniuses had trouble with mathematics. Among them were Benjamin Franklin, Pablo Picasso, and Carl Jung.

Winston Churchill could not get into Oxford or Cambridge because of his difficulty with Latin. Richard Wagner played truant from school because of his trouble with Latin verbs.

This is not to say, parents, that if your child is having trouble in school it is a sign that he is a genius. You should continue to look into areas where your child is having difficulty. I have included excerpts from this study merely to remind you that many people are late bloomers. Some children work best in a non-structured environment. For some there is a developmental lag and they catch up later. But for all our children there is hope where there is love.

JANUARY CURRICULUM CALENDAR

1—New Year's Day. Anticipate this day by asking children what they think "turning over a new leaf" means. Discuss New Year's resolutions.

6—Three Kings Day. Important holiday if you have Puerto Rican pupils. Epiphany—Greek Orthodox and Protestant holiday.

7—Russian Christmas. Check current calendar. Feast of St. John the Baptist—Greek Orthodox.

11—"Ashura." Islamic fast day commemorating the death of the grandson of Mohammed.

13—Stephen Foster's Birthday. Discuss the old South as compared to the present South.

15—Martin Luther King Day. Help students learn more about this leader. What was his dream? Talk about non-violence as a philosophy.

17—Benjamin Franklin's birthday. Have a class "Poor Richard Club" meeting like the one that convenes in Philadelphia every year on this day. Point out Franklin's many accomplishments.

31—Chinese New Year. Display some books about Chinese children, such as *May May* by Leo Politi (Scribner) and *Chinese in America* by Claire Jones (Lerner). Display some pictures of the Chinese New Year celebration, including the dancing animals.

Chapter 6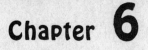

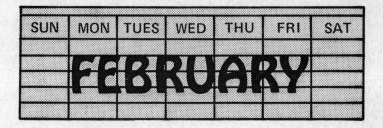

How to make your messages readable

Who are you writing for? When you write an article for a PTA newsletter, does it sound like a graduate course term paper? You would be surprised at the reading level that your local newspaper aims at. The average American reads at a ninth-grade level, although many persons read at a lower level. Most reading experts agree that people feel most comfortable reading at a level that is a notch or two below their maximum.

It is essential that you keep this in mind when you write a message for your teachers, parents, school board members, or student population.

Writing authority Robert Gunning has created a readability test that you can apply to your messages. The test is applied to a 100-word sampling. Count the average number of words per sentence. Count the number of words with three or more syllables. Add these two numbers. Multiply your answer by one half. The final result is roughly equivalent to a grade level in reading.

For example, if in your sample the average sentence length was 16 words and you had eight long words of three or more syllables, the sum would be 24. Half of 24 is 12, and so the 100-word sample would be written for someone who reads roughly on the 12th-grade level.

Gunning has found that writing samples for such magazines as *Harper's* and *The Atlantic* consistently score an average of 12. Samples from *True Confessions* weigh in at about 7; comic books are at the bottom with an average score of 6.

The result of this test for your district or school publications should be around 9 or 10. It certainly shouldn't go above 12, even if your district is loaded with college graduates. If you apply the test to what you are writing and find it scoring above 12, do something about it. Here are some tips for lowering the readability level of your written messages:

1. Reduce the average number of words per sentence to around 15. This doesn't mean that every sentence should contain 15 words. Aim for an average of 15. Start some sentences with an important action word. This eliminates unnecessary little words and sparks your writing.

2. Knock out the stilted pedagogical language. This will eliminate or reduce the number of multi-syllable words.

3. Keep the reader in mind. (Notice how we started this sentence with a key word; this is a five-word sentence that would have *less* impact if we made it 15 words.) Sadly, too many publications intended for community residents seem to be written to impress the superintendent, principal, board, or faculty. Scholarly writing can be avoided if all articles for community publications (and staff messages) are rigidly edited. This includes the superintendent's column and the board president's message. It is obvious in many publications that articles have been prepared by many hands and printed just as submitted.

4. People frequently read your messages while preoccupied with other duties. Such messages are not meant to be studied in a library, so keep them a year or two below the level of the reader!

Planning a successful school science fair

For some parents, the worst part of the school year is the time when their children come home with an announcement about the school science fair. The child feels some pressure to participate but is waiting for the parents to give ideas or actually help in the execution of a project.

You can avoid this annual hassle by insisting that your teachers accept only those projects that are a natural outgrowth of the classroom science lessons. In this way, every pupil is exposed to the same stimuli and should be able to go off and do something on his or her own.

In one affluent suburb, it became increasingly obvious that parents were actually preparing the sophisticated science fair projects at home and the only real input from the child came when he or she carried a project into the school building. This district then insisted that all projects would have to be done in the school building with some teacher supervision. Another district went the other route: it sent home guidelines for parents and solicited their help. Their projects then competed in such areas as Mother-Daughter, Father-Daughter, Mother-Son, etc. These were frankly projects that parents had helped with. The children were quizzed on their understanding of the elements of science involved. It was the amount of insight that won the prize, and not the glossy looking project.

Here are some criteria for analyzing elementary and intermediate school science fair projects:

1. Is a problem being investigated?
2. Is it a problem to which children can discover the answer?
3. If the project is an experiment, is it properly controlled?
   - Is it one problem or at least one problem at a time?
   - Are the findings reliable? Can they be repeated?
   - Were the findings quantified wherever possible?
   - Was the experiment repeated several times or done by several groups in order to secure as large a number of samples as possible?
   - Is the conclusion justifiable based on the findings?
4. Can you think of ways to extend or open-end the project?
5. Can you think of a more interesting and dramatic way to present the findings as a science fair project?
6. Is the project suitable for the grade at which it was done?
7. Could the project have stemmed from classwork?
8. Is the project one in which the children might have a strong interest?
9. Have safety factors been checked (glass, electricity, sharp objects)?

There will be times when you will want to check the pupils' concepts of their projects. This is very important when you are considering two or more candidates for first prize. Here are some typical questions you may wish to ask:

1. Why did you select this particular idea for your project?
2. What apparatus did you borrow or purchase? Which did you make?
3. How much time did you put into this project? Over how long a period did you work?
4. What books did you consult? Which people did you talk to?
5. Can you show us the original records of the data you collected?
6. What, if anything, would you do differently if you were to begin again?

As a judge of a science fair you should follow some cues. First, disregard the elaborateness of purchased items. Consider only the appropriateness of the materials used. Second, give all exhibitors an equal chance to make their presentations. Tell them that they will each have two minutes to describe the project. Do NOT interrupt during this time. Do not, by your questions or comments after the pupil presentation, give any evaluation of the project as compared to others. Do not discuss the exhibit or project in the pupils' presence. Form your own judgment before you confer with the other judges.

To help you use a standard or yardstick approach, try giving a score to each science project you judge. For example, list each project on lineá paper. Across the top, head five columns: Concept x 3, Method x 3, Technique, Format, Interview x 2, Total. Give scores in each box, i.e., 1=poor, 2=fair, 3=good, 4=fine, 5=excellent. Multiply these scores by one, two, or three. For example, an excellent concept would be worth 15 (5x3), or a good interview would be worth 6 (3x2).

One of the most delightful experiences is to hold a separate science fair for Grade One pupils. They love making things that move or displays of collections, such as rocks or leaves. Invite parents to come in and view the displays. Use a "show and tell" approach instead of an interview with pupils to check their understanding of their project. Many fine concepts will be learned from such a sharing experience. By all means, allow the first-graders an opportunity to view the upper school science fair first so that they can get ideas and inspiration. You may want to suggest that your teachers prepare an experience chart with the pupils after they visit the gym or other site to see your school science fair.

How good is your school security?

Is your building safe from intruders? Can unfamiliar visitors wander through the building unchallenged? In these parlous times it is best to beef up the security of your building. To do this you will need the cooperation of many people. Take a look at the comprehensive security plan described here. Pay particular attention to the variety of people that are involved in it.

After meeting with teachers, the Union chapter chairman, the custodian, and representatives of the PTA, the following school security plan has been formulated:

School Plant

1. The custodian will lock all doors from the outside, except the main entrance, every morning at 9:15 A.M. This will still permit the doors to be opened from the inside. Signs directing visitors to the General Office will be provided.
2. Visitors will be asked to sign a visitors' book stating their name, destination, and time of entrance and exit. Teachers will ask each visitor for a pass. They will ask any visitor who has no pass to obtain one in the General Office or at the lobby desk.
3. School aides or a parent-volunteer will staff this desk, located just inside the main entrance. Both intercom and an outside telephone line will be available for their use.
4. The supervisory and custodial staff will periodically check doors to see that they are in a closed and locked position.
5. Teachers have been asked not to be in the building before 8:00 AM or after 4:30 PM except when some after-school center activity is taking place.
6. The school public address system will be checked daily.
7. Mr. Barclay, vice-principal, is the authorized representative in charge of safety when the principal is absent. Teacher alternates' names are posted in the General Office.

8. Upon suspicion that an intruder is in the building, a coded message will be broadcast: "Miss Smith, report to the Auditorium." This will alert teachers to lock their doors. The last word of the message will indicate where the principal or his delegate can be found for further instructions.
9. When classes are in session, pupils will use only Staircase 2 to go on errands. This will give us only one staircase to supervise throughout the day.
10. Unfamiliar visitors will be announced in the General Office by intercom telephone.
11. School property (A-V, athletic, music) will be marked with the school name, using an electric stylus or indelible ink.
12. First aid kits will be checked weekly by the nurse. Fire extinguishers will be checked monthly by the custodian.

Staff

1. All teachers are aware of the school safety plan as well as the emergency fire drill signals and procedures.
2. Time at the February Faculty Conference was used for this purpose.
3. Teachers will keep all bulletins concerning emergency drills together in a folder available for reference and for a substitute to follow.
4. Periodically, teachers will review with their pupils basic safety measures (correct entrances and exits, restroom rules) and emergency signals and procedures.
5. Teachers will report any intruder to the office.
6. The principal will remove the intruder from the school building. Police will be called if necessary.
7. The lunch and custodial staff have been informed of our safety procedures.
8. Whistles are available for teachers requesting them.

Pupils

1. All children are instructed in procedures for safety and emergency drill signals by their teachers.
2. Children are trained to return to their classroom when signals are sounded.
3. Pupils are instructed as to which entrances and exits they are to use during morning, lunch, and afternoon hours.

4. In a non-threatening way, pupils are instructed by their teachers to avoid contact with strangers that they may encounter near the school.

Parents and Community

1. Parents are asked to have their children arrive in school at or after 8:30 AM. There is no supervision available before that hour.
2. Parents have provided the school with a completed Home Contact card which includes basic data including their telephone at work, a neighbor's phone, and their physician's name.
3. Community safety and health personnel (police, fire, hospital) have been consulted in formulating school safety plans.
4. Building inspections are made periodically by the Fire Department and Building Department teams.
5. The PTA executive board was involved in formulating the safety plan and preparing the Home Contact Card.

Bomb Scare Procedures

- Upon receipt of a bomb threat, by telephone or otherwise, the recipient should immediately notify the head of the school. The information will then, without delay, be forwarded to the Police emergency number—911.
- Particular emphasis should be placed on retaining the exact wording of the original message, and, if verbal, whether it was a male or female voice.

Demonstrations and Disorders

- All entrances to the building will be locked in the event of such an occurrence.
- All outside physical education classes will be cancelled.
- Teachers will remain with their classes and await instructions from the principal.
- If necessary, the police will be called.

What can we do for high school seniors?

At this time of year, the beginning of the second half of the senior year, many high school seniors develop "senioritis." They know their final averages have been computed. They have already been accepted or rejected by admission officers and they no longer see the relevancy of their courses.

High schools across the country are finding cures for this crippling "disease." These range from early graduation and college courses in high school to apprenticeships and independent study projects. What the programs share is an attempt to make the curriculum more flexible and challenging. In many cases the programs take the seniors out of the school building. In all cases the cooperation of teachers and parents in planning is of paramount importance.

An apprenticeship or work-study program is an increasingly popular option, particularly for those not going to college. Students work part time, usually for no pay, with professionals or craftsmen in a variety of fields. Some students use the opportunity to seek out a variety of careers. The National Institute of Education developed the "Experience-Based Career Education Program." Here students pick a career area that interests them, like health, banking, or law and justice. A student in law and justice, for example, works one or two days a week helping an officer at police headquarters, interviewing victims at the district attorney's office or perhaps following a civil case at a private law firm. After this 12-week "exploring" phase, a student can pick one job to work on for the next 12 weeks. At the end, a student has both a "feel" for many aspects of a career field and an in-depth knowledge of one.

A real "hands-on" approach is called "Walkabout," a system of learning in which pupils walk about in the world of work. It requires students to meet challenges in five areas: adventure, creativity, service, practical skill and logical inquiry. Experiences must be real, not vicarious or simulated, and must develop self-reliance, responsibility and confidence. In North Central High School in suburban Indianapolis a senior might work with a florist on a botany project, interview a state senator for a study of government, or do independent research on the city's housing patterns. Some students took field trips to Washington, D.C. for a firsthand study of government, and to Florida to study the ecosystem of the Everglades. More detailed information about "Walkabout" can be obtained by writing to Phi Delta Kappa, Box 789, Bloomington, Indiana 47401.

The high school in Baldwin, New York offers 60 college credits to its qualified seniors. The program began because seniors were stagnating and because no colleges nearby permitted easy commuting. The principal worked with Syracuse University in upstate New York to set up some courses. All courses are taught by the high school's teachers who are prepared in summer workshops run by Syracuse. Tuition for a three-hour course is $50.00— substantially less than that at most colleges—and all courses are accredited by Syracuse University. Among the benefits is the chance for marginal college-prep students to get a better picture of their abilities.

How to conduct a parent rap session

As a school administrator you have probably noticed that during the dark days of winter and just before the long awaited spring vacation, parent complaints escalate. There is no magic answer in this chapter on how to eliminate this natural concern of parents for their children's welfare. Sometimes, however, we can avoid over-concerns about situations that do not really exist. Many parents stop attending PTA meetings at this time of year. The days are short, the nights are cold, the roads are icy—you know the excuses. For many parents the PTA meetings no longer meet their needs. They do not want to get up and speak before a large group. They are tired of listening to those parents who do enjoy this kind of ego trip.

One way to get more parents back to school at night to discuss positive feelings is to conduct a rap session. In your flyer, announce an opportunity for parents to meet in *small* groups of six or eight to discuss school problems. The idea of small groups will appeal to many parents. Suggest to your PTA leadership that a member of the executive board sit in on each group. In this way, a more knowledgeable parent will be present at each group session. You should make it your business to circulate among the groups that night and act as a kind of resource person. Answer questions and give factual replies to their questions.

After a half hour or more of the small-group discussion ask one person from each group to report to the large group on their discussion. This reporter should be a volunteer. If no one volunteers, move on to another group. Using this technique, more parents will feel they have a forum.

Tips on supervising your teachers painlessly

In spite of your efforts to free yourself from a watchdog image, the observation of lessons remains a bugaboo for many teachers. Sadly, this attitude remains because supervisors have been identified with ratings, promotion, tenure, and salary increases.

To help change these attitudes we are suggesting a model of supervision consisting of four basic components that have been tested under experimental conditions. It is called "interaction supervision" by Robert Schwimmer, a Brooklyn, New York principal.

1. Interaction supervision is a method where feelings as well as content are the ingredients in establishing an interpersonal relationship between a supervisor and a teacher or a group of teachers. This relationship is grounded in Carl Rogers' design for developing a helping relationship. If the supervisor can provide a certain type of relationship, the supervisee will discover within himself or herself the capacity to use that relationship for growth and change. Only then will personal development occur.

2. Added to this philosophy is the mutual setting of yearly goals by supervisor and teacher, goals which are periodically reviewed and revised.

3. There is also a series of supervisory tools (observations, demonstrations, team teaching, conferences), which are used cooperatively.

4. Finally, there are the brief, personal-professional encounters between supervisor and teacher, which are fostered by the supervisor.

In the implementation of this process all four components must be in operation if we are to call it "interaction supervision."

You as the supervisor of instruction must feel that you are a "helper," a "facilitator," and a "catalytic agent." You must feel comfortable in that role. You begin to do this when you are willing to relinquish your role as supervisor in a strictly *boss* sense and begin to accept a more mutual colleague role.

All teacher-supervisor conferences must contain certain basic ingredients if interaction supervision is to be successful. These ingredients are:

1) There should be equal "giving" by teacher and supervisor. This is not a passive but rather an active relationship. Teacher involvement must be encouraged. It is a meeting of two professionals concerned not with superficial niceties but dealing realistically with educational issues, people, personalities and feelings.
2) Such a relationship in order to be growth-promoting must be based upon honesty, forthrightness, and concern for each other.
3) Conferences other than of the impromptu variety should be planned and should revolve around a problem to be mutually solved. In this way each member feels that the meeting was worthwhile and will thus set the format for future meetings.
4) It is the supervisor's job to set the tone of informality at these meetings. He or she is there to help as one colleague to another, not a doctor to dispense medicine or wisdom.

The group or grade conference should be planned around a topic of mutual concern and preferably in the form of a problem to be solved. The involvement of a maximum number of teachers who are concerned with the problem in the planning, conducting and evaluating of the conference is a must.

Throughout, the supervisor is a participant, resource, and mediator, but he or she is not to dominate, sway, or control.

What to do when head lice strike

Pediculosis, or head lice, is a condition that affects all strata of our society. It can no longer be said that only unclean children or lower economic class children are affected by head lice. Because it is so contagious, just one infected youngster can cause havoc in an entire school. Frequently the lice are transmitted from one child to another when hats are exchanged or combs used by more than one child. But this is not the only way. Hatless children can have lice move from the coat of an infected student to their coat collars in the coat closet.

As soon as one or more cases have been detected it is your responsibility to inform other parents. This is not a matter that will go away if ignored. We suggest you send home to all the parents a letter modeled after Figure 6-1.

Dear Parents:

There has been some incidence of Pediculosis (head lice) among the children in our school. Head lice are much more common in children than in adults. We are examining the hair of each pupil and will be excluding from school for treatment those who are found to be affected. It is expected that a temporary exclusion coupled with home treatment along the lines of those outlined below will be successful in ending any cases. Excluded pupils will be returned to school after treatment and inspection of the hair and scalp show elimination of the lice.

WHAT TO LOOK FOR

Small, white dandruff-like pieces which attach to the hair. If it is dandruff, the white will brush off and blow off. Head lice cling to the hair shaft and will not blow off.

TREATMENT

There are several good commercial products for the treatment of this condition. They include Kwell, A-200, Cuprex, and Del. All can be obtained at most drug stores and are used like a simple shampoo. The shampoo should be repeated after 4-7 days. Hairbrushes that have been in contact with infected hair should be boiled; clothing or hats should be dry cleaned or laundered and thoroughly dried in a dryer. The hair of all family members should be checked.

BE CAREFUL

Protect the eyes while treating to avoid irritation. The preparation used in treating head lice may be harmful if taken into the mouth. Keep it out of the reach of children. NEVER USE GASOLINE OR KEROSENE for treatment. Such use is highly dangerous.

RETURN TO SCHOOL

Your child may return to school as soon as he or she has no more lice or nits in his or her hair.

Please understand that we have found only a few cases among our children. This is no reflection in any way upon a person's personal hygiene or cleanliness. This condition is found frequently at this

FIGURE 6-1

time of year because children wear scarves and hats to school. It can be picked up in any place upon contact with a person having such a condition.

Thank you for your cooperation.

Sincerely,

Edmund Carter
Principal

FIGURE 6-1 (continued)

Because you may have some Spanish-speaking children who need to take this information home in their native language we are including an abstract of the above letter in Spanish:

Examine la cabez de cada miembro de la familia; en caso que se encuentre a alguien mas con piojos o liendres, empiecese immediatamente el tratamiento del cabello y cuero cabelludo, pues como bien saben, el piojo se pega.

Cuando en la escuela se descubre que una nina or nino tiene piojos, liendres orgranos en la cabeza, immediatamente se envia al hogar para que se someta al tratamiento que indicamos. Compre en la farmacia alguna preparacion para matar piojos y liendres, pues hay muchos remedios eficaces (Kwell, A-200, Cuprex, y Del).

Sample conference notes

STAFF CONFERENCE
February 23, 19____

I.   Administration.

     1.1   Pupil Health: Talk by Mrs. Nelson, School Nurse. Topic: Head lice.

     1.2   Dental Clinic: Free dental care is available for our pupils at the North Shore Dental Clinic on Tuesdays and Thursdays. Please inform the office of pupils who need an appointment.

     1.3   Kindergarten and Grade One: There will be a parent-teacher conference on March 4 and 5.

1.4   Grades Two-Six: Spring afternoon conferences will be held on Tuesday, March 14.

1.5   Report Cards: Distributed to pupils on Tuesday, March 12. Report cards are due in Supervisor's office on Thursday, March 7.

1.6   Spring Cleanup: Begin now to throw out obsolete or dated materials.

II.   Supervision.

2.1   Photographers: The PTA has arranged to have the pupils' pictures taken on Wednesday, March 15. Writing contest details to follow. Remind pupils the day before. Staff picture will be taken at 12 Noon.

2.2   Reading Comprehension Materials: A collection of new practice materials will be displayed and discussed by Miss Beane. Questions from all staff members are welcome.

III. Teacher Ventilation.

The grade leader for each grade will present his or her grade goals for the year. All staff members will react. Suggestions for future staff conferences will be explored.

From the Principal's Desk

By this time, you have seen your child's second report card. A comparison with his or her first report card and a talk with his or her teacher shows that_____is not doing as well as he or she is able to do.

If there is no improvement for the rest of the year, he/she may be held over next year.

It would help_____if you would have a talk with the teacher. Mr. Barrett, our guidance counselor, will also be happy to meet with you after you speak to your child's teacher. You may reach him at 716-5960.

Please contact___(Teacher)___to arrange an appointment as soon as possible. With parent-teacher-child cooperation and significant improvement your child can, at this point, move ahead to the next grade. If there is not significant improvement he/she will have to repeat the grade.

Yours truly,

Dennis Harper
Principal

FEBRUARY CURRICULUM CALENDAR

1—National Freedom Day. Commemorates the day in 1865 when President Lincoln signed a bill outlawing slavery. Have pupils write about the freedoms they enjoy. Discuss the restrictions that all of us have on our freedoms. What responsibilities does freedom carry with it?

1-7—National Children's Dental Health Week. Ask dental hygienist to talk to the pupils in Assembly. Arrange with local dental society to get samples and literature from toothpaste companies.

8-15—Black History Week. Consult *The Black Experience in Children's Books,* compiled by Augusta Baker for the New York Public Library. This is a bibliography featuring a rich variety of materials.

12—Lincoln's Birthday. Select a sound filmstrip on the life of Lincoln. Emphasize the deep concern that President Lincoln had for saving the Union. How many of these concerns still exist today?

14—St. Valentine's Day. Do some research into the background of this fun day. You will find some interesting conjectures on the real St. Valentine. Relate your activities to a fund-raising project for the local Heart Fund. They will love you for it.

15—Susan B. Anthony Day. Read about the life of this famous American who was born on this day. If she were alive today what would be some of her concerns?

22—Washington's Birthday. Focus on Mount Vernon. What kind of life style did George Washington enjoy? What were some of his activities when home at Mount Vernon? Compare the architecture of this building to that of other well-known residences.

Chapter 7

SUN	MON	TUES	WED	THU	FRI	SAT
		MARCH				

March can be a trying month for school administrators. Both children and teachers begin to anticipate the spring vacation. The short, dim days of winter are still with you. Pupils eating lunch in school have not been able to get outside because of inclement weather. The list of patience-tryers is endless. Yet March offers many opportunities for sparking the imagination of students and staff. For example...

Vitalize your approach to Earth Day

More and more of your students are aware of the ecology movement and share the concern of those Americans who want to save our environment. You will get a host of ideas from this letter (Figure 7-1) that one Staten Island principal sent to his teachers, exhorting them to involve their classes in celebration of Earth Day or Ecology Day.

Dear Teachers:

Welcome to the first day of spring. On March 20 at 1:13 P.M. (Eastern Standard Time), the moment at which the vernal equinox occurs, or the spring season begins astronomically, we will also celebrate EARTH DAY.

FIGURE 7-1

135

An EARTH HOUR, from 1:13 to 3:13 P.M., will initiate the DAY. The hour will begin and end with the sound of the United Nation's Peace Bell to be broadcast by radio around the world.

In preparation for Earth Day you should begin to plan NOW events to precede, take place on, and follow the March 20th date. As a guide, I have prepared the following list of suggested activities:

1. Prepare graphic displays on environmental problems, energy needs, food needs, housing, land use, living things in the city, population, recycling, transportation needs, and waters around us.
2. Survey and record the sources that contribute to the pollution of the school neighborhood.
3. Survey and record the sources that contribute to pollution in the homes. Map out and take steps to eliminate these sources.
4. Present assembly programs to demonstrate the science of measuring and checking pollution.
5. Post reports of pollution levels on bulletin boards.
6. Prepare exhibits on the effects of pollution on living things.
7. Have classes write and present plays related to one or more aspects of Earth Day.
8. Distribute seeds and seedlings for pupils to plant and care for.
9. Plant trees as symbols of renewal.
10. Organize pupils into Volunteer Air Pollution Observator and Reporter (VAPOR) squads to keep track of and work to eliminate neighborhood sources of pollution.
11. Set up anti-litter squads to campaign for cleaner streets.
12. Publish an anti-pollution bulletin. Give specific steps that parents and pupils can take to reduce pollution at home, at school, and in the neighborhood.
13. Arrange visits to aquaria, botanic gardens, environmental centers, museums, parks, wildlife sanctuaries and zoos.
14. Draw posters or write compositions on such themes as:
    The Wonder of Life
    Pollution—Spoiler of Life
    What I Can Do to Stop Pollution

Earth Day (Ecology Day) provides us with an unusual opportunity to raise the level of pupil awareness and understanding of the fact that people, and only people, can guarantee that Planet Earth will remain hospitable for generations to come.

Yours truly,

Charles Beadle

Sizing up your pupils' health status

March is traditionally the month when medical examinations are due for pupils going on to high school or entering kindergarten. It is best to start with a letter to parents (like the one in Figure 7-2, for example) requesting that they have their child seen by a doctor.

Dear Parent:

To protect your child's health in school, he or she needs to have medical examinations at certain times during his or her school career, and to receive protective immunizations against disease. The requirements and recommendations of the Department of Health are listed below.

Your family doctor is the best person to do the examinations. Please have your doctor complete the "Health History" and "Medical Report" below when he examines your child and gives any necessary immunizations.

If you prefer, you may have your child's medical examination and the necessary immunizations done at school. In this case, you yourself should complete the "Health History" below, and sign the other side of this form to request the services.

Health History

Dates

Successful Smallpox Vaccination
Diptheria-Tetanus or DPT
Polio: Salk Injections
        Oral Monovalent
        Oral Trivalent
Measles Vaccine
Rubella (German Measles)
Tuberculin Test
BCG Vaccination
Mumps

Has the child had any of the following conditions? Check.

___Chicken Pox   ___Frequent Colds   ___Heart Trouble
___Measles   ___Ear Infections   ___Vision Defect
___Rubella   ___Allergies   ___Hearing Difficulty

___Mumps   ___Convulsions   ___TB
___Rheumatic Fever___Orthopedic Defect ___Other

The following health services are recommended as minimal:

Immunization against poliomyelitis (required by law).

Measles vaccine if child has not already been protected by having measles.

Rubella—for newly admitted children under age eleven.

Diptheria-Tetanus-Pertussi immunization.

For new admissions in kindergarten and first grade only—a skin test for tuberculosis and an annual chest X-Ray if the test is positive.

In the fourth grade—a complete examination.

Pre-high school—a complete examination plus a booster for DPT and a skin test for TB.

If you do not have a family doctor, and wish these services to be given to your child in school, sign this form:

─ ─ ─ ─ ─ ─ ─ ─ ─ ─ ─ ─ ─

I request that my child be given the health services for his present grade, described above.

_____ _____ _____
Signature of Parent   Address   Date

IMPORTANT: Smallpox vaccination must not be given while the child or anyone in the household has eczema or a skin rash. Does your child or anyone in your home have eczema or a rash?

FIGURE 7-2 (continued)

Your primary source of health status information in school is the classroom teacher. As the budget squeeze worsens, there will be less nurse and medical service available to schools. For this reason it is important that you keep your teachers vigilant and encourage them to report on their pupils' health status. The letter in Figure 7-3 can be adapted to meet your school's needs.

TO THE TEACHER:

In order to ensure early medical attention for health problems among your pupils, you are asked to report below any known or suspected deviations from normal health, which in your opinion should have the attention of the school doctor or nurse. Include information you have received from parents or from the children themselves, as well as your own classroom observations.

Do not include simple vision problems and dental caries, which are separately reported. Do observe and report on:

rate of growth	drowsiness or lethargy
posture and gait	restlessness or irritability
speech	accidents
appearance and use of eyes	unexplained drop in academic
hearing and ears	work
condition of skin	excessive use of lavatory

Include any other items which seem to you significant, and put the report in the nurse's mailbox. The nurse will give these reports her immediate attention, and will confer with you on individual children as necessary.

Class_____ Room_____ Teacher_____

Child's Name   Health Problem

_____   _____
_____   _____
_____   _____
_____   _____
_____   _____

FIGURE 7-3

The letter in Figure 7-4 can be adapted for use in informing parents of the importance of dental care:

Dear Parents:

Good dental care is essential to your child's health. For those who cannot afford to go to a private dentist, our Health Department provides free dental care at the Springfield Health Center. Children whose parents have Medicaid cards are eligible for treatment privately or at the clinic. Such Medicaid children receive priority for treatment at the Springfield Center.

If you cannot afford private dental care for your child, please return the attached note to your child's teacher, requesting treatment. You will then be contacted by the dental hygienist. She will arrange an appointment for you to come to the clinic with your child to sign the necessary dental forms before treatment can be given.

You must accompany your child for the first visit. This is a rule of the Springfield Health Center.

Yours truly,

Jane Jenken
Principal

— — — — — — — — — — — — — — — — — —

Dear Ms. Jenken:

_____ I have received your letter regarding the Springfield Health Center Dental Clinic. I request that my child receive this free service.

_____ I have a Medicaid card and want my child treated at the Springfield Dental Clinic.

I understand that I must go with my child for his first visit.

_____   _____   _____
Child's Name   Class   Parent's Signature

_____
Home Address

FIGURE 7-4

How to maximize a teacher-nurse conference

The school nurse performs an important function in your school. You can maximize her efficiency by arranging once each year a teacher-nurse conference. During this time the two professionals can discuss potential and actual health problems of the children in your school. Figure 7-5 presents a form letter that one nurse we know sends out to teachers with the approval of the school's principal.

Dear Miss Petersen:

Our conference is on_____ at_____ AM/PM. Before the conference:

1. Read the District Office bulletin on health conferences.
2. Plan ways to keep your class busy for about 30 minutes.
3. Make certain that there is a health card for every pupil.
4. Check to see that you have entered the height and weight.
5. Have scholastic records and roll book available for reference.
6. Review cards to discuss the following items.

During the conference we will discuss:

1. Children without important immunizations.
2. Unusual symptoms.
3. Emotional problems surfacing.
4. Frequent absences for the same reason or a variety of reasons.
5. Complaints of aches and pains.
6. Unusual hearing or vision problems.
7. Family health problems that may affect your pupils.
8. Other symptoms or signs you have noticed in your daily contact with your pupils.

After the conference:

1. Make a notation that a conference was held.
2. Refer pupils or parents to a clinic if that is the recommendation.

Sincerely,
Janet Busch, R.N.

FIGURE 7-5

Making the most of a Career Day

More and more parents and teachers realize that the school has a responsibility to prepare its students, regardless of level, for the world of work. A very effective way to do this is to set up a Career Day program. In its simplest terms, this is an occasion when people from the community, representing different job categories, come into the school to talk to pupils in a structured way. We suggest some structure rather than just a rambling spiel on the part of the local banker, lawyer, or machinist.

Your major responsibilities will be to select and invite the careerists and make sure that they keep their date. The scheduling of the pupils is relatively simple. Some administrators assign a room to each speaker and have the pupils go from room to room depending on their individual interest. For younger children you may want to avoid their traveling through the halls and instead have the speakers go to their classrooms. This would narrow down their freedom of choice, however.

A letter from an elementary guidance counselor to the teachers in his school is shown in Figure 7-6.

Ladies and Gentlemen:

The time draws near. Tuesday at 9:00 A.M. promptly, please start your class on their way to their first occupation. Encourage them to move quickly and directly through the halls. I have programmed their 3" x 5" preference slips to give them all of their choices, but at the same time to distribute the load on the guest equally over the three half-hour periods.

Please insist that your students abide by the large red figure on their slips, e.g.:

- Large red #1 on a slip for Fireman means *9:00* in Room 114.
- Large red #2 on a slip for Dentist means *9:30* in Room 116.
- Large red #3 on a slip for Baker means *10:00* in Room 117.

During the half-hour period, no one may switch rooms.

There have been a few changes in the assignment of rooms, so please go over all the room assignments as per the new schedule with your class and tell them to write the room number on their preference slips. Tell them to have the appropriate slip ready to give to the presenter as they enter the room, as a sort of admission ticket. This will help us see how many pupils attended each room. We will not attempt to take attendance or tally, but the admission ticket should give us a good measure of control.

Use your judgment as to when you will give out the slips. Some classes will lose them if they are handed out on Monday. If you think you will have time before 9:00 A.M. on Tuesday, that would probably be the better time. A few pupils will not have slips due to

FIGURE 7-6

their absence last week. I have provided a few blank slips in your class set for their use. They will not be numerous enough to upset the balance in each room.

As a follow-up may I suggest that you have a discussion and sharing time after 10:30 A.M.? I think there will be an urge to share and a need to ventilate a bit, and all can benefit beyond the three experiences they have had. Make no promises, but a few of our guests have already talked of follow-up field visits, etc.

Daniel Miller
Counselor

FIGURE 7-6 (continued)

For intermediate and senior high school Career Days you may decide on evening meetings. Many parents like to attend these programs and you can attract a larger audience at night. These older pupils need more time and their wide range of interests requires more room space than the day school can afford to relinquish.

In order to help these more mature pupils zero in on their career choice, some schools ask the pupils to prepare a simple career paper. After narrowing his or her job interests to five fields, the student then selects the one field he or she wants to look into as a possible career choice. The result of this investigation is a paper that includes the material in the following outline:

1. Job title
2. Preparation
   A. Educational
   B. Personal
3. Employment
   A. Type of work
   B. People with whom you would work
   C. Possible places where employment can be found
4. Job requirements
   A. Hours
   B. Physical requirements
   C. Mental requirements
5. Occupational rewards
   A. Salary
   B. Advancement
   C. Personal satisfaction

6. Personal disadvantages
7. Advantages
8. Summary: Why is this job for you? Why is it NOT for you?

No doubt you have found that most young people are quite undecided about career goals. You can help them arrive at a better understanding of themselves in the area of job satisfaction if you have your students fill out a simple questionnaire like the one seen in Figure 7-7.

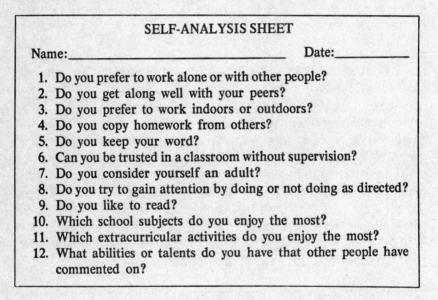

FIGURE 7-7

Such a self-analysis sheet will help your students discover more about themselves, their interests and their futures. It can be incorporated into a social studies or English curriculum.

Tips for holding a worthwhile Book Fair

There are times when every administrator wishes he could have a larger petty cash fund. At other times he or she wishes that the pupils in his or her school valued books more. You can satisfy both wishes by running an annual book fair. The letter to parents presented in Figure 7-8 is self-explanatory:

Dear Parents:

Our school is going to have a BOOK FAIR on Thursday, March 21 in the gymnasium. Classes will be scheduled to visit the display of books and pupils will be able to take home the books they purchase. No orders will be taken.

Building their own library is a wonderful experience for children. It is our wish that each child in the school will be the proud owner of one or more paper-back books—personally selected and treasured. Prices begin at 35c and go up to $2.00. Classes from kindergarten through Grade 6 will be visiting the BOOK FAIR.

Parents are invited to visit the BOOK FAIR and make selections also. All money collected will be deposited the same day.

Yours truly,
Helen Kelly
Principal

FIGURE 7-8

A careful study of the letter in Figure 7-8 will reveal some good tips that you can use in your school. Book vendors like to send you sample books and then have you take orders. This is better for them. We have found that using a vendor who will send you a variety of books on approval with the right to return the unsold books is better. The pupils prefer to take the book home with them. They can select the precise copy they want. They do not have to wait two weeks and then get a slightly frayed copy. In two weeks, their tastes may change.

Notice that this principal is inviting the entire school to the book fair. Kindergarten age is not too young to start a love of books. Be sure you have a selection of easy-to-read picture books for kindergarteners. There are a great many inexpensive ones on the market for them today.

It is a good idea to invite parents to come to the book fair. They love handling the books and frequently make selections for birthday presents. Also invite the custodial and kitchen staff. They enjoy being part of the total school and they all have nephews and nieces to buy books for.

This letter tells the reader that all money collected will be deposited the same day at the bank. This tells anyone with an idea of breaking into the building that night for the proceeds that it would be a waste of time. Some schools suffer a break-in every time they hold such a special fund-raiser. This one line inserted in the letter may preclude such an untoward event.

Most vendors will pay you 20% of the gross sales. This can be a nice source of petty cash for you for the entire year. Do give suggestions to the supplier regarding the kinds of books that you think will do well in your school.

How to improve the way you order textbooks

Selecting the best instructional materials for your money is a time-consuming and complex task. Yet, as the price of paper goes up, the cost of textbooks soars. For many of us the annual allotment of funds for books remains the same and so we must be sure we are not ordering books that are not going to be used effectively. This is especially true in the selection of books for your reading program. To make the job of evaluation easier we have prepared this checklist. To use it, respond to each statement with either "yes" or "no."

1. Procedures for helping the teacher decide when students are ready to use the materials are included.
2. Tests for pupils' achievement are included.
3. There are clues for diagnosing reading difficulty.
4. The publisher has a reputation of responsibility and service.
5. Some other administrator has used these materials and I can contact him or her for an unbiased opinion.
6. Skills are sequenced appropriately, introduced carefully, and reviewed periodically.
7. Vocabulary and interest level are suitable for the pupils using the books.
8. The content of these materials will stimulate and challenge students without frustrating them.
9. The experiences presented in the materials are appropriate for students in this school/school district, and this community.
10. Information is presented in a fair and impartial way.
11. The materials are not too large, bulky, or complex.
12. Training of teachers is available.
13. The price of the materials is reasonable and within the budget.

14. Adequate teacher manuals or guides are provided at no cost.
15. These materials do what they are intended to do better than any other materials I know of.

Occasionally you and your staff may want to change the basal reading system you are using in favor of another. This can be a traumatic experience in some schools. The first question that some teachers will ask is, "Why change?" This is especially true if they are familiar with the old series and they generally fear the unknown. You and the more progressive members of your staff can point out some of the advantages for change: getting out of a rut, handling newer story lines, capitalizing on later research findings in reading, a lift for the teacher.

Here is how one school moved from one basic reading series to another over a two-year period:

Winter—
- Obtained sample sets.
- Sets distributed to Grade 1 teachers.
- New series reported on at Grade 1 conference.
- Decision made to introduce new series into two classes.

Spring—
- New series shown and discussed with executive board of PTA.
- Executive board volunteered to finance one class.
- School financed second class on first grade.
- New series discussed with general membership of PTA.
- Teachers selected for next year who will use new series.

Fall—
- Instruction began.
- Reading consultant worked with teachers in October.
- Conferences held between principal and participating teachers.
- Inter-visitations held by first-grade teachers.

Spring—
- Progress reports to PTA.
- Administered reading achievement tests.
- Conferences with participating first-grade teachers.
- Began working with two selected second-grade teachers.
- Selection of pupils for these four classes.

Fall—
- Reviewed results of tests and teacher judgment.
- Met with four teachers using new series.
- Pre-selected two third-grade teachers for next year.

Spring—
- Evaluated program so far. Involved teacher using old series.
- Ordered enough books for eight classes next year.

You can see that this administrator proceeded slowly and cautiously. He involved interested teachers and parents. The new series was monitored carefully and the pupils measured to see if they were gaining from the new series before it was introduced on a larger scale.

It is important that the teachers in your school feel that they have a voice in the selection of instructional materials. One way to do this is to have your custodian build a bookcase in the teachers' lunchroom or restroom. As publishers' samples arrive in the mail, stack them in the teachers' lunchroom or work room. Call attention to the new sample books in your conference notes. Ask teachers to drop a note in your mailbox advising of some book that they favor in particular. You may want to mimeograph a textbook preference sheet that you hand out to teachers just before books are to be ordered. Invite them to respond, and use their preferences when you order.

Talk to your teachers informally about textbooks. All teachers have opinions about the instructional materials they are using. They will be only too happy to tell you how they feel about the books in their rooms. You have by now learned to take their comments with a grain of salt. The important thing is that you listen to them. Of course, some will gripe about any books and others will succeed with the most archaic materials. Your job is to see that every teacher has suitable materials with which to work.

If you are sometimes annoyed by the arrival of a textbook salesman you can turn such an unexpected call into a public relations plus. Find a teacher who is free at that time and invite him or her to sit in with you as the salesman goes through his pitch. The teacher will ask practical questions, and even more important, the teacher will feel elated to be part of this experience. Again, you have a more global view of the school and you can't order every book that each teacher likes. By setting up a small textbook-ordering committee of teachers you can show them firsthand how you have to stretch the textbook dollar.

Guidelines for conserving paper

For the next few years we can expect to wait longer for deliveries of paper and pay more for paper goods. As a result of this shortage and for ecological reasons too, it is necessary to make more effective use of paper. The following suggestions are passed along to you:

1. In mimeographing, use both sides when possible.
2. Re-use file folders.
3. Use short paper (8 1/2 x 11) whenever possible.
4. Try to combine multiple announcements into one notice.
5. Make only the number of copies necessary.
6. If surplus one-sided copies are available, use the reverse side for scrap paper.
7. Order yellow paper for seat work instead of white when possible.
8. Re-acquaint teachers with the use of the chalk board instead of ditto sheets for routine work.

Your approach to teacher negotiations

As a school administrator you are frequently asked to participate in contract negotiations. These meetings are frequently like a socio-drama or role-playing activity. Each participant assumes a role. The partisan feelings of teachers and taxpayers are portrayed by their representatives onstage or around a conference table. All negotiators have some awareness of their responsibilities to their constitutents. As the school administrator you are usually asked to record the minutes. Since tempers sometimes get hot at these sessions, no one wants a verbatim account. Everyone does want a sober, accurate account to look back upon.

If you are asked to make notations, include the following:

1. The date, time, and place of the meeting, and a list of the participants actually present.
2. A simple, accurate statement of the issue or issues under discussion.

3. A brief resume of each viewpoint expressed and the name of the speaker.
4. Items that are agreed upon.
5. Items where agreement failed.
6. Postponement dates, including time and place of next meeting.
7. Signatures of both chief negotiators attesting to the accuracy of the minutes.
8. Your signature and title.

Avoid the temptation to "leak" some of the table talk to one of your favorite teachers when you get to school the next morning. This is a trap that many principals fall into. They are so eager to impress their teachers with their skill and charm as a negotiator that they spill confidential material prematurely. This may impress the teacher-listener at first, but soon you will gain the reputation of a "talker" and will not be asked to participate in any important district-wide matters again.

Also avoid the temptation of inserting your own opinions where they are not sought. We know how smart you are in the area of labor and management. Don't tell us unless we ask. Some principals describe the tone of their schools as if they were working in the Garden of Eden. A more objective view finds pockets of discontent and rotting apples. Assume your assigned role at the negotiation table and do not overstep it.

Making the most of grievance procedures

When a child gets a fever it is a warning signal that some infection is present. Without the fever the illness might go undetected until it became very serious. In modern school contractual agreements, the grievance procedures serve a similar warning purpose. Make the most of these procedures so that discontent does not fester and worsen in your school.

A grievance procedure is an essential safety valve for letting off steam. It is a device by which a teacher or other employee indicates that he or she wants his or her "gripe" taken seriously by management. As with all upward communication initiated by the teacher, grievances should be processed without undue delay and promptly resolved, when it is in your power to do so. Every effort should be made to reach a settlement before the grievance is committed to writing—or if it is already written, before it goes to the next level.

Listening at grievance hearings requires the highest level of your listening skill. In such a situation you need the ability to listen to the words and the meanings *behind* the words. Here are some tips for such face-to-face listening:

1. Establish a "climate" for good listening, i.e., a reputation for giving a teacher a fair chance to be heard without prejudging, or impatience, or recriminations. This "rep" is not achieved by reiterating, "My office door is always open." It is achieved by a deserved reputation for courtesy and consideration.

2. Show a genuine interest as you listen. A comfortable chair should be in a face-to-face location. An ashtray should be handy. Avoid showing impatience by rocking your swivel chair or tapping your pencil.

3. At first, listen with a minimum of interruption. Later, probe for facts and feelings but don't argue. Let him (or her) "get it off his (or her) chest." When the teacher has spoken, restate his or her position to his or her satisfaction. Make notes of all the facts and tell him or her that you will check the situation. If this has already been done, state your findings.

4. If the teacher or other employee seems to be holding in his or her feelings, try to learn what these are and how deeply they run by asking, "What is your reaction to....?" or "How do you feel about....?" Most questions are safe enough to ask, but watch out for the loaded questions—"What's the excuse this time for coming late?"

5. Try to determine what the underlying cause is behind an employee's complaint or grievance. His or her initial beef may be only a symptom of a deeper dissatisfaction, either in school or at home.

6. If you can't give the teacher an immediate answer, tell him or her when he or she can expect an answer. Delaying an answer gives you time to check facts, to consult district policy and to "sleep on" your tentative first reaction. If the final answer to a teacher's complaint or grievance is "No," explain the reasons and try to get the teacher to accept them. To help him or her adjust give some harmless concession if this is possible.

7. If you are conducting a meeting of a group of teachers and one person seems to have a lot more on his or her "chest," schedule a talk with him or her alone. He or she might have something important to say but feels embarassed in the group. Even more important, sometimes a teacher will say something in a group that he or she might not say to you alone. This might be something fresh or sarcastic, and the teacher is trying to impress his or her colleagues.

8. Don't allow the occasional ear-bender or the aggressive individual to make you forget your listening techniques or tarnish your reputation for sympathetic listening. Keep your temper and allow him or her time to tell his or her story and to receive a prompt answer.

9. Remember—listening is the more important half of oral communications, and, "You ain't learnin' nothin' when you're talkin'."

Sample conference notes

STAFF CONFERENCE
March 26, 19____

I. Administration.

    1.1   Career Education Summer Institute: Mr. Erwin, Guidance Counselor.

    1.2   Teacher Preference Sheets: Send to the office your class and grade preferences for next year.

    1.3   Book Fair (see attached schedule): Please encourage your pupils to buy at least one book on Thursday, March 29. There will be no ordering. Pupils will take their selections with them. All money will be deposited at the bank on Thursday. No money will be left in school overnight.

    1.4   Sabbatical Leaves: Applications for leaves beginning August 1, 19__must be in the District Office by April 1. This information is available from Mrs. Diego.

    1.5   Bathroom: Grades 1 and 2 pupils who are taken to morning recess should not have to be excused to use the bathroom again during the morning. Please discourage this unless a special medical problem exists.

II. Supervision.

2.1   Reading Tests: These will be given on April 2 and 3. Each teacher will administer tests to his or her own class. Review the test manual with special emphasis on timing of sub-tests. Some classes may have to complete name grid on a day prior to taking the actual test.

2.2   Earth Day Follow-up: The efforts and many projects on the part of our teachers have attracted much favorable comment. We expect to have the school garden rototilled to loosen up the soil. Areas will then be available for classes to plant in.

III. Safety and Security.

3.1   Do not leave money in school overnight.

3.2   Contact school aides when you have finished using the movie projector. They will lock it up.

3.3   Be sure to lock your classroom at 12 Noon and at 3:00 P.M.

3.4   At appropriate times tell pupils that money collected in school is always deposited in the bank on the same day. Some schools have had break-ins on the day of collections for weekly lunch money and special events.

From the Principal's Desk

Ah, but a man's reach should exceed his grasp, Or what's a heaven for?

Robert Browning

This quote is especially appropriate when we consider our school's Career Night which will be held in the school Gym next Thursday evening at 7:30 P.M. The world of work and the vast array of careers available to our children as future occupations can't possibly be comprehended in one night. We are dramatizing through this one night the importance of career education.

We can't wait for the future since it is here now. We should prepare for it as educators, parents and students. We should focus our thinking on preparing our youth for selecting a combination of courses that will prepare them for professional careers in fields of work, commensurate with their interests, which have economic growth possibilities. The subjects they would study would not just be learning for learning's sake, but would bear directly and specifically on their planned careers. This would thoroughly motivate them and help students who may now not be too successful in school because they don't see their subjects in a functional manner.

Our Career Night is only the beginning—a giant first step. We can help them along the way. Be sure to attend.

Bernard W. Alfred
Principal

MARCH CURRICULUM CALENDAR

5—Crispus Attucks Day. Explore the role of Black people in colonial times.

Second Week—Girl Scout Week. Discuss terms "Brownie," "Intermediate," and "Senior Scouts." Tell story of Juliette Low of Savannah, Georgia. Look up scouting in encyclopedia.

9—Amerigo Vespucci's Birthday. Recall events of other Italian navigators and explorers.

14—Prophet's Birthday. Islamic holiday. Use wall map and trace countries of the Middle East.

17—St. Patrick's Day. Prepare hall bulletin boards.

Fourth Week—National Poison Prevention Week. Prepare units in health education classes.

Usually in March: Jewish holiday of Purim—Story of Queen Esther. Annunciation of Virgin Mary—Greek Orthodox.

Chapter 8

SUN	MON	TUES	WED	THU	FRI	SAT
		APRIL				

This is usually the month when school administrators get news concerning their new contracts. Sometimes April is the month when you learn that your contract is *not* going to be renewed. The initial shock frequently brings emotional swings from outrage to depression. During this vulnerable period you may do something, or fail to do something, that could harm your future in school administration. We would like to suggest...

What to do if your contract is not renewed

We are concerned about the personal judgments a school administrator may make during this critical time and are including a list of caveats or warnings of things you should NOT do at this time.

1. *Don't resign.* You may want the satisfaction of saying, "Keep your job, I quit." But this is a luxury you can't afford. Later is could be the source of real problems by ending any claim you might otherwise have for reinstatement and lessening your leverage in any subsequent contract discussions.

2. *Don't make threats.* This may turn your few supporters against you. Threats smack of an intemperate use of power, which all school boards members generally resist. A threat carried out loses the good will others may hold for you. A threat unfulfilled makes one look impotent. You may find yourself working with some of these people in another capacity in the future.

3. *Don't sign anything.* A hastily drafted termination settlement document or an involuntary or coerced resignation is
hardly ever in the best interests of the school administrator. Once a
compromise agreement or resignation is signed and accepted by the
school board it is often too late for the administrator to reopen
discussion of such vital matters as payment for unused vacation,
continuation of hospitalization coverage, retirement or annuity
payments, or termination pay.

4. *Avoid the newspapers.* In most towns and cities, the school
administrator is a public figure. Sometimes a school administrator
looks upon an attempt to dismiss him or her as a blow to local
public education. Even though this may be the case, holding a press
conference or visiting the editorial offices of a local newspaper in an
agitated personal state can be disastrous. If you succumb to this
temptation the dismissal becomes a "hot item," and a quiet settlement, fair to you and your family, is politically impossible.
Because you involved the media, the board now feels it must save
face and keep a hard line in their dealings with you. Similar
reasoning applies to the immediate involvement of PTA, advisory
groups, or citizens' committees in your troubles.

5. *Avoid the blues.* Even if the dismissal sticks, you are not
the first school administrator ever fired. Termination does not
necessarily mean that you are inadequate. It could very well be
exactly the opposite. Don't let the school board, or a portion of it,
shatter your self-confidence. This may yet turn out to be the best
thing that happened to you.

What are some positive steps you can take? By all means
contact your attorney. You have valuable legal rights stemming
from federal or state law or your employment contract. Don't trust
your knowledge of school law to save the day. Do invest in a good
lawyer. It is best to bring legal counsel into play at the very
beginning.

Be sure to contact your professional association at once! Your
association leaders and staff have had considerable experience
dealing with the delicate and sensitive situation you face. Listen to
their advice. They are on your side. Under some circumstances,
your association will be able to provide you with assistance in
paying legal fees. At the least they will be able to recommend a few

lawyers from whom you can make your own choice. They can also be of help in suggesting the best kind of agreement you should make with the lawyer of your choice.

And now for something more mundane...

How to transform graffiti into murals

Roberto was dragged into the principal's office by the custodian. The custodian had the boy's collar in one hand and an aerosol can of spray paint in the other. The boy was obviously the phantom sprayer who had been defacing the rear of our brick building with elaborate "art deco" style signatures, such as "Pancho-77" and "Viva." After some questioning we learned that Roberto had been a bus graffiti expert, inscribing his signature as far and wide as possible.

The immediate problem facing the custodian was how to cover this impossible-to-remove graffiti. The principal thought of setting up a group of artists to paint a mural over the slogans and ornate names. This mural project had many positive outcomes: the wall was no longer a disgrace, Roberto found a positive outlet for his urge to paint, and the school neighborhood became an integral part of the school, literally and figuratively.

Under the supervision of the art teacher, the group toured the neighborhood and took black and white photos and color slides of the community surrounding the school. They also looked through books containing urban pictures. The art teacher kept a log. Excerpts of this log will help you follow her plan, step by step.

It was time now to put something on paper. We began by projecting our photographs and slides onto large sheets of paper we taped on the wall. Using slide projectors and an opaque projector for pictures from books, we traced the projected images onto the paper on the wall.

Some of us measured and taped while others emphasized lines on the collage drawing and tightened the composition. Then we taped clear acetate over the drawing and drew a grid of lines spaced three inches apart, forming a 3" x 3" square over our design. We numbered our vertical lines and lettered our horizontal lines so that we could duplicate our design on the wall, section by section.

Meanwhile, an outdoor team washed the wall of the building with white paint. The pace and excitement accelerated as we started working on the actual wall. The group was generally accepting and supportive of everyone's contribution. It had never doubted Roberto's ability. He and his friends assumed the role of the bodyguard to the mural when it was complete. It was a huge street scene. It depicted the neighborhood around the school in a favorable light. The community looked upon the wall as a landmark rather than an eyesore.

What if a child does fail in school work?

Examples of warning letters to parents of children who fail are presented in Figure 8-1.

Dear Mrs._____:

At the present time, in spite of our efforts, your child's work in class indicates that he/she may have to repeat Grade__next year. Please discuss with the teacher what you can do to effect sufficient improvement by June to permit his/her promotion.

We have attached some thoughts on homework which may be of help. But, above all, see your child's teacher.

Very truly yours,

Burton Williams
Principal

— — — — — — — — — — — — — —

Please detach and return to school

Dear Mr. Williams

I have read your letter and I understand that my child_____ is in danger of being held over in June.

_____ _____
Parent's Signature   Date

Dear_____:

Your son/daughter_____is not doing as well in school as he/she can. Mrs. Keyes, your son's/daughter's teacher, is quite concerned as I am. At the present time it looks as if_____will not be promoted in June.

FIGURE 8-1

By working together, perhaps we can see a marked improvement in the next three months. I have asked Ms. Seaford, the Guidance Counselor, to talk with you. She will be calling you for an appointment. I look forward to meeting with you and Mrs. Keyes and Ms. Seaford some day next week. Thank you for your cooperation.

Sincerely,

Edna Vreeland
Principal

FIGURE 8-1 (continued)

Providing "help sheets" for parents

Frequently parents will ask how they can help their child at home in a given subject. These requests are especially popular at this time of year when June rolls into sight. Almost always this request comes from an intense interest in and a sincere desire to aid the progress of the child. A wise administrator has a supply of "help sheets" available to give such a parent when the request is made. Here are some suggestions for helping children at home in the areas of reading, arithmetic, and homework.

HOW A PARENT CAN HELP AT HOME—READING

1. Make your house a house of books; if you are a TV bug rather than a reader, you child is likely to be one, too.
2. Start with books that center around your child's interest—sports, airplanes, boats, construction kits, etc.
3. You did not get upset because the neighbor's child got a tooth before yours. Remember—reading skills are not all developed at the same time.
4. Introduce your child to the library. But if the library is to be of lasting value to him, you must use it, too.
5. Give books as gifts for birthdays, Christmas, and so on.
6. Find a place in your home for your youngster to keep his books.
7. Do not send the child on an errand as soon as he sits down with a book.
8. Encourage your child to tell you about what he has read.
9. Find the time to discuss stories with him. Tell him about books you are reading.

10. Praise your child for his efforts. Compliment him on the progress made and not necessarily on the level reached.

11. Encourage your child to share his knowledge of reading with a younger child. Nothing will turn a youngster on more to reading than assuming the role of reading teacher.

12. Subscribe to a children's magazine. There are many good ones available today. Your child will look forward to his own mail and reading material.

13. Supply words your child does not know when he reads to you. Do this objectively without any comment. Do not appear annoyed if he stumbles on a word you helped him with before.

14. If you feel you must drill your child on certain words, make simple flash cards out of paper. Reward him for words he masters. Show him concrete examples of his "learning" by enumerating the words he knows. Have him tear up the word cards he no longer needs.

15. Enjoy the process. Let your child know that you do not mind helping him. Don't make your child feel that reading with him is just as painful for you.

Dear Parent:

Many times parents ask us about the "new" math. It scares them and keeps them from helping their children at home. While the textbooks and other learning materials we use do contain new approaches, the fact remains that 2 plus 2 still equals 4. Here are some suggestions for helping your child at home feel more comfortable and successful with numbers:

1. Let your child help you to:

   — double-check your register tape from the supermarket.
   — find your train on the timetable.
   — help measure for a do-it-yourself project.
   — figure cooking recipes.
   — keep track of oil, gas, mileage on trips.
   — plan the route on a road map.
   — check the temperature.
   — read the barometer.
   — help make out bank deposit slips.
   — check your cancelled checks with you.
   — go over floor plans of new house or carpeting purchase.

2. Give him or her numbers in play times, such as:

   — puzzle books and dominoes
   — quick mental drills with number facts

— card games involving numbers
— word puzzles involving number concepts

3. Don't pass your dislike for mathematics on to your child; you will solve nothing by telling him or her that you "hated fractions," or "math is for boys."

4. Help him or her see ways in which math is used in the modern world:

   — making tall buildings stand up
   — rockets, jets, and space flights
   — banking and insurance careers
   — computer technology

5. Help your child understand big numbers:

   — how big is a million?
   — how long would it take to count to a billion?
   — how far away is the moon?
   — how long ago was "a thousand yesterdays"?
   — how do we write "a thousand thousands"?

6. Help him or her solve simple problems. Help your child learn to estimate or approximate answers. This will avoid ridiculous responses.

Sincerely yours,

Dr. Elizabeth Raymond
Principal

Dear Parents:

Here are some thoughts on parent help at home—homework.

The purpose of homework is to extend and reinforce what has been learned in class and to develop a sense of self-discipline, personal responsibility, and independent thinking.

We at the John Tyler Elementary School encourage parents to:

— show a positive interest in their children's homework as well as their school work.
— cooperate with the teacher to make homework more effective.
— provide children with a suitable place to do homework, away from TV or pre-school children.

—serve as consultants about assignments, but not to do the assignments for the child.

—see that assignments are completed neatly.

—encourage but not pressure children.

—talk to their children about their attitudes toward school work and homework.

In the interest of variety and in order to give pupils an opportunity to develop different kinds of skills, not all assignments will necessarily be *written* assignments. Some will be to read, to interview, to cut out, to collect, *to study*, to do research, to listen to a particular radio program or watch a special TV program.

Our school policy is, generally, not to give homework on weekends. Reason: to allow pupils to engage more fully in family activities.

Please feel free to consult your child's teacher whenever there is a question about homework. We want homework to be a help and not a punishment.

Yours truly,

Felix Romero
Principal

How to avoid the pitfalls inherent in testing

The use of standardized test results is becoming a political football. Some city fathers are using test scores to make major policy decisions about education. In these days of declining pupil enrollment, test scores may play a part in determining which teachers are hired and which teachers lose their jobs. They already affect when students graduate and in what manner. They may determine which school districts get state or federal money and how much.

We as administrators have a job to do. That job is to tell parent and citizen groups the whole story regarding testing. We must place standardized testing in perspective. It is not like body temperature or a bank statement. Point out the whole constellation of factors that affect an individual pupil's performance on a given test on a single day.

It is up to us to make sure that everybody on the staff understands what the testing program is all about and what the scores mean. The first briefing should take place early—when the tests are given—followed by a detailed explanation of the scores when they are tabulated, but before they are released to the public. Think how your faculty would feel if they read the test scores in the evening paper before getting the results in school.

When we say the staff, we mean *everybody*—the secretary who answers the phone and the school nurse who chats with a neighbor under the hair dryer. To friends and casual acquaintances, they work for the school and their opinions carry a lot of weight.

This is not to say that teachers or others should respond with, "Test scores don't mean anything." This threatens the school's creditability. To a parent, test scores mean a lot. Downplaying their importance will look like an effort to evade responsibility. What we should do is present the score and then interpret what a single score means. Also point out the many aspects of reading achievement that a test cannot measure, such as love of reading, types of books read, and an appreciation of literature. Give some support to parents who talk about the child who was coming down with a cold on the day of testing or the tensions in a home where the father recently walked out.

Test scores may influence teacher expectations regarding student potential. Teachers getting records of pupils with high scores have a certain expectation of these pupils. Records of pupils with low scores usually provide the teacher with a different kind of mind set, even before they lay eyes on the child. Robert Rosenthal and Lenore Jacobson wrote *Pygmalion in the Classroom,* a book in which they reported their experiment with bogus record cards. When they gave a teacher fictitious information about a pupil's ability, the actual achievement of the child in that teacher's class reflected the teacher's initial expectation. When teachers were told in advance that they were getting some high-achieving pupils (who actually were merely average or less), the teachers treated the pupils as such and the pupils achieved above grade level.

In order to produce valid and reliable results the test itself must be administered accurately. Here is a memo that one principal issues his teachers prior to actual testing.

PROCEDURES FOR ADMINISTERING THE TESTS

1. Before the test:
   - After clocking in on Tuesday morning, pick up from Mrs. Santoro—
     - 1 package of tests and answer sheets
     - 1 box of pencils
     - 1 stopwatch
   - Place on outside of classroom door a sign reading, "Testing today, do not enter."

2. During the test:
   - Keep a record of the time for the test on the chalk board.
   - Do not allow children to leave the room after the test has begun.
   - Be an active proctor. Walk around the room but do not disturb the pupils.

3. After the test:
   - Collect booklets and check them for completeness, including the identifying data on the cover sheet.
   - Write names of absentees on the outside of the brown envelope.
   - Alphabetize the answer sheets—boys and girls separately.
   - Return test, pencils, and stopwatch—personally.
   - Arrangements will be made by the office to test absentees.

Handling student rights and responsibilities

For the past decade principals have been badgered with the issue of pupil rights, especially in the senior high school. Not as much emphasis has been placed on the opposite side of the coin—pupil responsibilities. This a job for us, the administrators. We have to point out that rights *and* responsibilities go hand in hand. We have surveyed what different school systems have been doing in this sensitive area and would like to report some good ideas to you.

The South Dakota Department of Public Instruction has a simple booklet with the "right" on one side and the related "responsibility" opposite it, to show the connection.

The South Carolina Community Relations Project developed a comic book, full of cartoons, illustrating rights and responsibilities in both a serious and a humorous vein.

In Pittsburgh, Pennsylvania, a faculty-student committee put out a facsimile of a driver's training instruction manual. The 24-page pocket-size booklet is called, "Your Right-of-Way Road Map." The rights are combined with the responsibilities to show the reader that one follows the other and that respect for both is required for an effective system.

The best way to come up with meaningful "responsibilities" is to have a cross-section of students write their own list. In Charleston, South Carolina, representatives from several high schools came together to hammer out some basic principles of conduct on which all could agree. After much brainstorming the students arrived at the following consensus statement:

> I will respect my fellow students, teachers, rules and regulations as I respect myself.
> I will communicate with others to help unite my school.
> I will help eliminate the use of violence as an answer to problems.
> I will demonstrate respect for my school building and campus.
> I will support my school's activities and organizations.
> I will display good sportsmanship and school spirit at all times.
> I will not complain about the problems in my school but will work to improve my school.

These statements were printed on pledge cards and distributed by the student council.

Such efforts do not put an end to all school disturbances, but they remind us that the troublesome students in any school are the minority, that most students are serious and dependable and given a chance can set the tone for the entire student body.

Your approach to Law Day

Every school has at least one lawyer in the PTA. You may even have a lawyer or a lawyer's spouse on your staff. Capitalize on this by instituting a Law Day celebration in conjunction with the national holiday that takes place this month in most states. This is a chance for your children to look at their rights. Here is an article that appeared in a PTA newsletter describing how one elementary school commemorated this occasion. You can easily adapt their program to an intermediate or senior high school.

> Law Day was celebrated at our school on April 29 with a special program for 5th- and 6th-graders. Attorney Carl North and Detective Jack Meeks, both P.S. 19 parents, and Bruce Regan, an Assistant District Attorney and a former P.S. 19 teacher, visited classrooms to conduct workshops and to participate in a mock trial.
>
> The visiting lawyers and detective were impressed with the children's questions and their responses to the issues of individual liberties and human rights. Preparation for role-playing and prior class discussion helped to make the experience more meaningful for the students.
>
> The script for the mock trials was based on an actual court case dealing with a student's right to due process of law prior to suspension from school. The jury of peers found that the student had been suspended without procedural due process. Discussions of constitutional rights and the legal ramifications were extended beyond the program time. The planned events served as a catalyst to further study.
>
> What a student gains from these kinds of activities is highly personal, depending to a great extent on his or her level of maturity and experience. For many students it was the first time they had thought about their rights as children and the protection afforded by the Constitution. It is during the middle childhood years that children begin to rationally examine concepts of morality, fairness, and the role of the individual in a democracy.
>
> Our thanks to our guests who helped vitalize our Law Day program. I think everyone who participated came away with a new respect for our rights as individuals in a democracy.

How to get the most out of your substitute teachers

April seems to be the time of year when teachers who had perfect or nearly perfect attendance all year begin to absent themselves from school. In some schools it is not easy to get substitute teachers. In all schools it is not easy to get good substitute teachers who take their day's work seriously and think of themselves as more than just glorified baby-sitters.

We have found that when you ask substitutes for a log of what they did *prior* to taking over the class, they start with a more positive mind set. Also, if you require your staff to leave a detailed lesson plan, you will not have a "wasted day" when the regular teacher is absent. See what you can do with this form at your school:

SUBSTITUTE TEACHER LOG

Class_____ Date_____

1. My name is:_____
2. Dates of coverage:_____
3. Curriculum areas of instruction:
    Reading:_____

    _____

    Math:_____

    _____

    Language Arts:_____

    _____

    Other:_____

    _____

4. Special activities:_____
5. Homework assigned:_____
6. Homework checked:_____
7. These pupils were especially helpful:_____
8. These pupils were problems (be specific):_____

    _____

9. Materials or notices distributed or collected:_____

    _____

10. Comments:_____

By all means make sure that you collect these forms at the end of the day. It is a good idea to collect them personally. Scrutinize the form briefly in the presence of the substitute teacher. In this way she or he will know that you take it seriously. Never give the substitute teacher the impression that as long as a warm body is in front of the class and the pupils are reasonably well behaved, you are satisfied.

Get your message across instantly

Does your intercom system buzz incessantly? Are teachers tired of having their lessons interrupted with public address system announcements? In Franklinville, New York, a resourceful principal—William Shubeck—found himself with the same irksome problems of message distribution that most schools have: "Mr. Lerner, report to the Guidance Office . . . Jill Smith—your mother brought your biology project; pick it up at the office . . . Basketball tonight—8:00 P.M. elementary gym . . ." and on and on.

Shubeck decided that a television message display system, similar to that used at airports to announce flight arrival and departure times, might be the answer. It could deliver a message and, at the same time, have the impact of a visual presentation. Within three months a home-constructed alpha-numeric video display system with typewriter unit was completed at a cost of $250.

The next step was to slightly modify the five obsolete 23-inch black and white television receivers to receive and display the generated messages and to accept a control signal for the on-off function and an F.M. audio signal for background corridor music. Installation was step three, and the new high school message system became a reality, at a total cost of only $500, with five wall-mounted receivers—one on each of three floors, one receiver in the combined cafeteria-study hall, and one receiver in the library-medical center.

If you were to take the time to add up the number of hours spent per year traveling to and from class with messages and the number of repeated announcements made, you would see how economical this system really is.

Complete plans for wiring your school for this kind of simple but effective message system can be obtained by writing to Mr. William Shubeck, Principal, Franklinville Junior/Senior High School, 31 North Main Street, Franklinville, New York 14737.

Sample conference notes

FACULTY CONFERENCE

April 28, 19___

I.   Administration.

     1.1   School Library Media Day, Wednesday, April 30.

     1.2   Conservation Day, Friday, April 25.

     1.3   Pupil suspense procedures.

     1.4   Science Fair—April 28 through May 2.

     1.5   School Board Elections—Tuesday, May 6. After-school and evening programs are suspended. NOTE: Political activity cannot be considered as "personal business" on this day.

     1.6   Registration of Kindergarten and first-grade children: May 5-16.

II.   Supervision.

     2.1   New Library acquisitions:
           Natural History Magazine
           Merit Student Encyclopedia

     2.2   Reports:
           Audio-visual—Mr. Gladstone
           Guidance—Miss Shaw
           Social Committee—Ms. Blackman

     2.3   Test Papers: Please send to the office one set of written English papers for your class. This can be composition, poetry, letter-writing, etc.

From the Principal's Desk (message for student handbook)

This handbook has been designed to give you and your families, in comparatively simple, concise form, a picture of our school, our activities, and our rules and regulations. Read through this handbook thoroughly. Familiarize yourselves with the various sections and the few, but important, regulations included.

With this handbook as your guide to the school, you should very quickly find your way in our building and in our varied school extracurricular activities. In this way, you too will become an important part of Curtis Intermediate School.

By participating in our activities, by joining those clubs and taking part in those programs in which you are interested, you will add to the pleasure you can get out of your stay at Curtis. At the same time you will achieve all the academic success you, your parents, and your teachers hope for.

With this handbook we of Curtis—the administration, the faculty, and the students—welcome you and wish you well for your years with us.

Sincerely yours,

Anthony Gaeta
Principal

APRIL CURRICULUM CALENDAR

First Week—National Library Week. Make sure that every pupil in your class has a library card. Plan a class trip to the library. Call ahead to see if you can show your class how books are accessioned and prepared for the shelves.

4—(varies with calendar) Han Shih Festival. Chinese holiday sometimes called Cold Food Feast. Point out that spaghetti and many other dishes had their origin in China.

5—Booker T. Washington's Birthday. Show filmstrip illustrating the hardships this great American overcame.

Annunciation of the Virgin Mary (date varies)—Russian Orthodox.

Second Week—Pan American Week (April 14 is Pan American Day). Bring in parents and other adults for a program depicting the many contributions made by North, Central, and South Americans to the quality of life in our hemisphere.

13—Thomas Jefferson's Birthday. Highlight this president's talent for invention.

17—Verrazano Day. Excellent opportunity to show role of Italian navigators in our country's development. Show picture of Verrazano Bridge in New York.

Passover—Jewish holiday that comes at different times in the spring. Commemorates the exodus of the Jews from Egypt.

23—William Shakespeare's Birthday. Trace development of English and American literature.

Chapter 9

SUN	MON	TUES	WED	THU	FRI	SAT
		MAY				

This is the time of year when interest sometimes begins to lag on the part of pupils and teachers. You have no doubt noticed how helpful it is to publish a list of year-end activities that everyone can look forward to. Such lists may contain items like Field Day, Flag Day, distribution of yearbooks, ordering of autograph albums for graduates, Awards Assembly, Kindergarten Graduation, trips to the new school, school picnic, dance fete, and Final Assembly. Just a listing of the dates and times of these activities can be like an injection of vitamin B-12 to the staff and students.

The teachers may be looking forward to next year and the kind of assignment they will have, so this is a good time to get out a "Teacher's Preference Sheet." In many cities these last few years have been hectic with budget cuts and last-minute changes in organization and allotments. Some years it seems as if the list of teachers for next year that we take home in June is not the same as the group of teachers we have on board just two or three months later. Nevertheless, teachers like to have a voice in the kind of class or classes they will be teaching in the fall, and so we suggest that you...

Make the most of a Teacher's Preference Sheet

It is usually a good idea to distribute these sheets as part of the May faculty conference notes. It can be a simple ditto or rexographed sheet, something like the one shown in Figure 9-1.

```
┌─────────────────────────────────────────────────────────────┐
│              TEACHER PREFERENCE SHEET    _____          │
│                                            Date              │
│                                                             │
│  Name:_____ │
│  Present assignment:_____ │
│  Class last year:_____ │
│  Assignment two years ago:_____ │
│  Preference for next year:_____ │
│  Leaves taken during the past three years:_____  │
│                                  Dates:_____    │
│                                Duration:_____   │
│  Comments:_____ │
│                              Teacher's Signature            │
│                                                             │
│  Please place in principal's mailbox by June 1.             │
└─────────────────────────────────────────────────────────────┘
```

FIGURE 9-1

With all our talk about participatory democracy, this is a concrete example of putting it into action. Let every teacher feel that he or she has a part in the assignment of classes. What is most important is that you do *not* merely hand these out without any explanation. By all means *do* explain some of the contractual and budgetary restrictions you face. Do point out the district policy on seniority and the likelihood of certain classes and programs being cut out of the school budget for next year. However, wherever possible you should take into account the preference of the teachers in making assignments.

Better ways to work with student-teachers

The schools are the only place where the beginning teacher can explore the many alternatives in methodology and planning under the careful guidance of a skilled teacher. No matter what the student-teacher's course work background is, there is no substitute for work in the classroom. Similarly, there is no better source of free and enthusiastic talent that you the administrator can find.

Some colleges merely "send" their student-teachers to you with some infrequent supervision on their part. You have a role to

172

play in their growth but you should not assume complete responsibility for them. In order to place your student-teachers properly you should know something about them *before* they arrive. Ask the college for a personal data form that will give you valuable background information of a personal and academic nature. You can then match him or her with a cooperating teacher who is likely to work well with the student-teacher.

Your student-teachers will want, of course, to become familiar with the classroom, teaching materials, pupils, and the school program as rapidly as possible. He or she needs to be supplied with all the books and other materials the pupils use, by whatever procedure is appropriate and approved in your school. But in addition, he or she wants to feel at home and to become a real part of your school, not just a visitor. You can assist greatly in this process by seeing that he or she meets all the teachers of the subject or grade during the first few days. Also, provide access to hand-books, manuals, or other bulletins about the school and school procedures. It will be most helpful if you can arrange some informal contacts early in the semester with special personnel (guidance, remedial). Lunching with a group of teachers may be the simplest way to start the process.

Each student-teacher needs to be shown where to put his or her wraps and materials, as well as to be assisted in finding a satisfactory place to work in lesson preparation, grading papers, preparing teaching materials, etc.

Student-teachers want to be helpful from the very beginning and their natural nervousness tends to disappear as soon as they get busy. Three different types of induction activities may help them to become actively involved at once and to develop readiness for full-responsibility teaching. Encourage your teachers to do the following with their student-teachers:

1. Assign routine activities. Prospective teachers need to learn about many routine matters—forms, records, and procedures; teachers should delegate some of these activities to student teachers from the very first day. A good general rule suggests that you assign to student-teachers responsibility for certain routines until they learn to do them efficiently, and then quickly assign different tasks. During sustained teaching, however, students usually carry all those routines that are a regular part of their total teaching

responsibility. These rather mechanical activities are a good way to get students involved almost at once, but the student-teacher should also move rather quickly into more responsible activities.

2. Utilize your "assistant." Helping the teacher with any activity where another adult is an aid can be profitable. For example, during the first few weeks your "assistant teacher" can write at the board, assist with demonstrations, check objective test papers, give elbow assistance to individual pupils during supervised study and other work sessions, and help a returned absentee make up his work.

3. Have them do "bit teaching." Most student-teachers write enough on the personal data sheet for you to pick out topics in which they are especially well prepared. This information may help you arrange for your student to serve as a resource person and become involved in "bit teaching"—give a special report; give a carefully prepared demonstration; conduct a drill; give an assignment; direct a committee project; or carry on any of a great many simple, unitary teaching activities of short duration. He or she may be of help in a bilingual program. The teacher remains in charge. He or she introduces the student at the appropriate time, and takes the class back again when the mini-lesson is over. A series of these "bit teaching" experiences of several different types is one of the best ways to get a student-teacher ready for regular full-period teaching. These activities have the advantage of being easier to plan, easier to execute, and often make possible some initial success as a foundation upon which to build more growth.

Don't feel guilty about "exploiting" student-teachers, or "taking advantage" of them. They are in your school to learn. The best way for them to learn is to "do." Of course, you can let them languish in the rear of a classroom taking notes, but this will not help them as much as the ideas we gave you above.

How to help teachers find jobs

In today's job market the need for teachers is shrinking. The baby boom is over, yet colleges are still turning out many graduates with majors in education. Because of district belt tightening, you may find yourself in a position where you are going to lose one or two of your least senior teachers next year. Here it is May and you

want to help these young people find a position for next year.
Besides sympathy and the slim hope that the cut positions will be
restored in the fall, you must offer them something concrete to go
on. These six suggestions should help you help your teachers. (The
first five are for the teacher; the sixth is for you, the administrator.)

1. If you are interested in teaching abroad in elementary and
secondary schools and summer seminars write to:

U.S. Department of Health, Education and Welfare
OFFICE OF EDUCATION
Washington, D.C. 20202

Ask this office to send you a copy of the latest edition of
"Opportunities Abroad for Teachers."

2. Every college library and many public libraries have a copy
of the following publication:

Patterson's American Education
Educational Directories Inc.
P.O. Box 199
Mount Prospect, Illinois 60056
Library Call Number REF. 1 901 P3.

This publication, which is revised yearly, presents information
about public school systems, private and denominational schools,
colleges, and universities. It also contains a full-page county outline
map of each of the 50 states to help in determining the location of
school systems, high schools, and other listed schools. By using a
road map, obtained at any gas station, you can select 100 towns in a
section of the state in which you wish to teach. Once you have
selected the towns or cities, you then will be able to get the proper
names and addresses of the superintendents from the Directory. At
this point you are ready to send a copy of your professional resume
and a cover letter inquiring about possible openings in the various
towns.

3. If the above suggestions are not productive, you may want
to register with a commercial teachers' agency. *Nota bene:* commercial agencies charge from five percent to seven percent of a
year's salary. Registration is binding for a period of two years. A
listing of these agencies can be found in the Education Section of
the *Sunday New York Times* or other large metropolitan
newspaper.

4. Many positions in education are obtained through personal contacts. It is recommended that teachers attend professional meetings where principals and superintendents are present. Attendance at social activities with school administrators is also desirable.

5. If you live near a large city, and still have not gotten a job by September, visit the parochial and private schools and speak to their principals. These schools are frequently in need of teachers since their pay scales are much lower than the public schools and they may not offer comparable fringe benefits. You needn't belong to the particular religious denomination of the parochial school to land a job.

6. As the teacher's present employer you can be of great help. Write a detailed letter of recommendation. Encourage the teacher to duplicate it. Call your fellow principals to see if they can use a good teacher. Don't bother trying to help a poor teacher get a job. There are too many good ones walking around. By all means, encourage your teacher to list you as a reference. Be sure to give your summer address and telephone number in case the new principal wants to call you before hiring him or her.

Should students help evaluate teachers?

Your first reaction to the above question is probably *no!* If you still doubt that students should have a role in evaluating teacher performance, take another look at the evidence. It strongly suggests that students can reliably evaluate teachers and that many teachers actually welcome constructive student criticism. In San Mateo, California, Kalamazoo, Michigan, and Montgomery County, Maryland, student evaluations are used in large measure. In these school systems formal evaluation programs have replaced the casual approach taken in the past. It wasn't so long ago when a self-confident teacher would do no more than ask his or her students to write an essay evaluating the course at the end of the year. Sometimes the principal would place a stack of mimeographed evaluation forms on his desk and invite teachers to submit them to their students. Usually the better teachers used the forms to pat themselves on the back and the less able teachers avoided them altogether.

The kind of evaluation we are talking about doesn't use the students as hatchetmen but does stress its aim—which is to raise the level of instruction. We urge you to make this program voluntary in your school, at least at the beginning. At San Mateo, where evaluation is a student government project with financial support from the district, only about half the teachers agreed to participate during the first semester. By the second semester the figure had jumped to 80 percent. Some of the comments reported were: "Teachers are really interested in what their students think of them." "As long as it is not a witch hunt...." "We welcome student feedback that is well organized and responsible."

Here are some of the questions that Montgomery County uses in their questionnaire. The students are asked to respond with a "Yes," "No," or "Don't know."

1. My teacher knows what I can do.
2. My teacher gives me work that is not too hard or too easy.
3. My teacher wants me to say what I think.
4. My teacher gives me enough time to finish my work.
5. My teacher explains things to me so that I can understand.
6. My teacher gives me fair grades.
7. My teacher gives me enough chances to show what I know.
8. My teacher makes the room look nice.
9. My teacher tells me when I do something good.
10. My teacher will help me with problems in and outside school.

If you would like to try this out at your school, we learned of a few good sources of evaluation forms you can buy for just a few dollars. Ask for the current price when you write.

"Students Rating Scale"
    Dr. Russell Eidsmoe
    Morningside College
    Sioux City, Iowa 51106

"Teacher Image Questionnaire"
    Dr. Rodney Roth
    School of Education
    Western Michigan University
    Kalamazoo, Michigan 49001

"Teacher Evaluation Scale"
University Bookstore
Purdue University
360 State Street
West Lafayette, Indiana 47906

Since teachers are most anxious to improve their skills and are genuinely interested in keeping alert to student feelings, you owe it to yourself and your staff to feel them out as to student evaluation in some form. They may opt to have a simple anonymous essay written by pupils at the end of the semester. If they are interested in seeing a more sophisticated form, write to the above institutions.

Getting the most out of driver education

What one single innovation kept an inner city school from erupting with pupil unrest? What is it that can make a 17-year-old girl with a 101° temperature want to come to school? The program is driver education. Its allure is universal.

We have heard a great deal about "self-motivation" on the part of students. This is particularly true in this subject. Cutting and truancy are practically unheard of in this department. The reasons are obvious. "Driver ed" opens up a whole new world for teen-agers. They can drive the family car earlier. Their insurance rates in most states are lowered. It gives them mobility. They actually leave the school grounds legitimately.

Whether the youngster is college bound or a potential dropout, driver ed offers a desired learning experience. Your grade advisers can use it as the carrot at the end of the stick. Offering the course later in the student's high school career provides motivation to learn.

There are ample opportunities to integrate driver ed with other strands of the curriculum. Reading a classic because some English teacher says it is good frequently is not enough to motivate a reluctant reader. However, put a driver ed manual under his nose and he will study it for hours. Handing him a reading list of related auto care books with author and call number will send him to the school libary in a hurry. Consumer education pamphlets dealing with car purchase and maintenance become popular reading projects.

Social studies teachers bemoan the fact that map skills don't seem to be taught in the lower schools anymore. Take a youngster who has just come from driver ed and hand him a home state map from a petroleum company and you have a captive audience. With the help of an overhead projector and some felt tip pens you have a virtual map laboratory.

Math teachers are fascinated at ⁺he way long division becomes important to some youngsters only after they discover that if you take the miles traveled and divide it by the number of gallons needed to fill the tank you get your miles per gallon. Math and math formulas become second nature to the serious driver ed student.

Few things will erase the stereotype of girls and their ineptitude with mechanical things more than a course in simple auto repair. In most schools this course attracts more girls than boys. If we are concerned about making our schools more relevant to the needs and interest of our pupils we must take another look at driver education. Perhaps there are other areas of real life experiences that we can bring under the umbrella of our high school curriculum.

Suggestions for implementing "Rights of Handicapped Children Week"

During the last few years we have seen a greater emphasis placed on the needs and aspirations of handicapped children. Many states commemorate the rights and responsibilities toward children with special needs during the month of May. Some school boards promulgate an official announcement such as this one:

WHEREAS, the Richmond School Board recognizes the rights of all children to receive a public education of high quality;

WHEREAS, this public education should enable children to achieve intellectual, emotional and physical growth;

WHEREAS, children with physical, mental and emotional handicaps to learning should receive adequate educational services;

WHEREAS, the special needs and rights of handicapped children have not been adequately explained to the public; and

WHEREAS, the Richmond School Board believes that these children should participate wherever possible in all school activities;

NOW THEREFORE, BE IT RESOLVED, that the Richmond School Board proclaims the week of May 12 through 19 as "Rights of Handicapped Children Week." The Superintendent, with his staff, is instructed to plan for that week a public education program concerning handicapped children.

There are many ways in which high school principals can implement such a proclamation. Displays, posters, exhibits and programs can be developed with the cooperation of the various supervisors of the Special Education programs. Speakers for staff conferences, PTA meetings, etc., may be arranged through the district office. Pupils on all levels should hold discussions about handicaps and how all people should relate to one another.

This is a good time to show the community the kinds of things that handicapped pupils can do well. Art shows and crafts fairs usually abound. One activity that has drawn a lot of attention recently is the Special Olympics. This is a bona fide competition of pupils in track and field. The only difference is that the pupils possess a variety of handicaps. This in no way dampens their enthusiasm.

Another popular activity is a musical concert with a band and/or chorus made up of pupils from special education classes. Of course, we should be aware of all our pupils all year long. However, it has a positive effect on these pupils when they shine on their own at some time during the year.

Focusing on the evaluation of supervisors

Whether you are a principal or a superintendent you are expected to evaluate supervisors as well as teachers. These may be vice-principals, assistant principals, department heads, subject area supervisors, or a host of other staff and line people. In some districts this evaluation takes the form of a new contract. In other districts, especially large cities, it may be a perfunctory rating form. Sometimes you, the administrator, are asked to write a narrative report on a supervisor. This is a little more difficult.

In order to help you rate your assistant more fairly and more comprehensively, we are giving you four broad areas that you *must* include. In addition, we are spelling out for you some of the major sub-topics you should cover in your report. By following our suggestions you will write an evaluation that will speak well for yourself as well as for the person you are evaluating.

A. Instructional and School Program Improvement: Consider, to the extent applicable, the supervisor's effectiveness in areas of curriculum, teacher training, instructional materials, meeting individual and group needs, motivating students to achieve, guidance, discipline, testing, co-curricular activities, health, etc.

B. Administration: Consider his or her effectiveness in planning, organizing, leading, follow-up, controlling, and establishing teamwork in administrative functions such as record-keeping, reports, correspondence, office management, security, plant, etc.

C. Staff Support: Consider effectiveness in selecting, training, evaluating and support of staff; in this regard consider objectivity, sensitivity, morale building, participation, incentives, firmness, cooperation, etc.

D. Relationships: Consider relations at all levels, i.e., pupils, parents, teachers, subordinates, supervisors, school board members, other departments or agencies, and professional organizations. Describe effect of involvement with community resources, parent organizations, and availability for consultations, grievances, guidance, etc.

After you have touched upon these four critical areas you will be able to give an overall performance rating. It is usually a good idea to have some kind of worksheet that you can hand the person you are about to evaluate. Ask him or her to fill it in and return it to you. This sheet would call for some items that you may no longer remember. For example, perhaps this vice-principal spent four weekends traveling with the district orchestra early in the school year. You may not have a written record of it and it may have slipped your mind. Surely it should be included in your report. The worksheet, which you would verify for yourself, is a valuable tool for avoiding hurt feelings and insuring thoroughness.

Tips for using audio-visual aids creatively

Upon reading some of your students' comments about the instructional program you will, no doubt, find that many of them comment favorably on their teacher's use of audio-visual aids. There are many ways to use A-V equipment other than instructional. The Seminole (Florida) High School offers these suggestions:

- Make a film to show new students the types of courses offered.
- Make a filmstrip to show parents of incoming students the program.
- Let the student council make a film to arouse student interest in their projects.
- Take photos of events where students are honored and present them to their parents.
- Videotape student interviews about school problems to show parent and community groups.

In Powell, Wyoming, each kindergarten parent had a chance to see his or her child in school activities, via videotape. Two TV sets were used so everyone could see what was happening on screen. After the showing, kindergarten teachers answered questions and arranged for individual parent conferences. The public relations gained by this idea was great. The entire school district has benefited from this event as the parents felt teachers were communicating with them.

You can use movie-making to motivate intermediate school age pupils. Poor readers find that they are able to record a story of their own creation without the use of the written word. Later, as they want to record comments made by peers, they are motivated to learn to spell key words correctly. When asked, they produce a plot outline of their story on paper, again reinforcing our need for fluency with the written word. The initial breakthrough is with film, and the recorded language in print follows. Being able to read the instructions regarding film loading convinced one 13-year-old boy that reading was more than just story books. He later re-wrote the camera's instructions in simple language for his less able classmates.

Your school should have more than just the dozen pupils of the AV Squad involved with media. Start with a Camera Club after school or a mini-course in Photography instead of the traditional art course. Slowly provide training for your teachers and then involve more and more pupils in taping, movie-making, taking snapshots, and using projectors. It will add another dimension to your communications objectives.

How to avoid conflict over contracts

One area of concern for administrators is the confusion that frequently accompanies teacher contracts that come due this month. Unfortunately, new contracts and the renewal of old contracts vary considerably from year to year and among teachers in the same district. Occasionally it becomes an area of conflict when one teacher finds out what is in someone else's contract.

This becomes more involved when oral agreements are not put in writing. A cardinal rule is to send confirming letters after any oral communications that promise jobs or imply costs, contracts, or that something will be done. These letters should be concise. They must not promise anything directly or indirectly beyond what was agreed to in the initial conversation. It is best to mail them within a day or two of the oral agreement. You should include a line asking the recipient to write you if any corrections are needed.

If you are hiring a teacher for the fall or for a summer program and the funds have not yet been approved, be sure to state: "...we have *tentatively* scheduled...based upon federal funding." This will avoid a law suit from the teacher who states that he or she was prepared to render service based on your letter.

In writing such a letter to a prospective teacher be sure that:

1. You refer to a specific phone conversation.
2. You describe the job specifically.
3. You state the possibility that funding will not materialize.
4. You give a date of final decision.
5. You request a written confirmation.

In general you will find that any correspondence concerning contracts should follow these rules:

1. Keep it simple and clear. A letter covering one topic can be easily filed. If it covers two or more topics it may be difficult to find when you want it.
2. State any limitations, uncertainties, or unusual contingencies before the close. Use a separate paragraph for this.
3. Do not hesitate to repeat certain important points if emphasis is necessary.
4. Include relevant district policy in your letter.
5. Letters going out after May 15 should include your summer mailing address, unless you pick your mail up every week.
6. Cultivate a lawyer friend. When something a little tricky comes up, give him or her a call.
7. Don't panic! Other administrators have had sticky situations come up before you. They will have problems with contracts after you retire. Just get good advice and take it. Too many administrators get good advice from top-flight, talented lawyers and then do the opposite because of some hunch or feeling they get. You will have trouble defending your hunches when the school board has paid counsel for advice.

Sample conference notes

STAFF CONFERENCE
Monday, May 24, 19____

"Don't be afraid to take a big step if one is indicated. You can't cross a chasm in two small jumps."

I. Administrative Items.

   1.1 Attendance Periods: Ninth attendance period ends on May 29. Total days this period—20. Total days to date—153.

   1.2 Pupil Attendance: Our school's percentage of attendance for April was 92.2%. We were the third best in the district.

   1.3 Clerical Half-Day—Thursday, June 17: Pupils will be dismissed at noon that day so that teachers can complete their clerical work.

   1.4 Record Keeping: Please be sure that all entries called for are made accurately and in the right places. Errors and omissions have been noticed on some cumulative record cards.

1.5 Plan Books: No formal collection of plan books will be made after June 18.

1.6 Instructional Materials: Samples of textbooks, etc., are on display in Mrs. Simms' office for your inspection. Teachers' requests will be taken into account when the book order is prepared. Please place your completed request form in my mailbox.

II. Instructional Items.

2.1 Summer Safety: Please conduct lessons dealing with water safety, treatment of sunburn and insect bites, bicycle safety, profitable ways of spending summer hours, etc. Bulletin boards on these themes are also appropriate.

2.2 Composition: Please give your pupils the opportunity to write a letter to next year's teacher telling about themselves and some of the activities they enjoyed in your room this year.

2.3 Guidance: If you have a pupil in your present class who was referred to any clinic or service but was not reached on the waiting list, please send his or her name and the agency's name to Mr. Milford.

From the Principal's Desk (for insertion in yearbook)

Dear Graduates:

Four years ago, you entered Eastern High School full of anticipation, expectation, and anxiety mixed with trepidation. Four years later, you leave high school with a great deal more sophistication, poise, and we hope marketable skills.

The staff at our school likes to feel that we have done a good deal in helping you along the way to full realization, not only in terms of educational growth, but also in terms of social and intellectual development.

Each of you has remembrances. I hope that most of them are pleasant. When I look over the list of graduates and recall your faces and accomplishments, I am most impressed with this class. You overcame many obstacles during your years at Eastern. When you were Sophomores our building modernization program began. We are in the final throes of it now. When you were Juniors the Jamestown River flooded the valley, and many of you performed heroically, giving assistance wherever needed. For some of you it was an adventure just getting to school during the aftermath of the flood.

It has been a joy for me to listen to your expressions relative to matters that were, at the moment, important. Student council meetings, advisory councils of other kinds and rap sessions with the various leadership elements of the school have led me to the conclusion that all is right with "our kids" even though all is not right with the world. You have a strong voice in shaping your future. Use your direction well, with intelligence and with consideration for other people. Stay with it! Look for little signs of progress. You will recognize them.

Sincerely,

Dr. Vivian Rosati
Principal

MAY CURRICULUM CALENDAR

1—Loyalty Day. Discuss concepts of patriotism and loyalty to family, country, and ideals.

1—Lei Day in Hawaii. Garlands of flowers are worn in our 50th state on this day as a symbol of good will and friendliness.

Month of May is Radio Month. Make a class survey of the number of hours each week each child listens to the radio. What kinds of programs are heard? What percentage of radio listening is to a car radio? A transistor?

Prepare for Mother's Day with a crafts project.

Second Week—Police Week. Emphasize positive aspects of a policeman's or policewoman's job.

Third Week—National Transportation Week and World Trade Week. Mention both in a discussion of man's interdependence on others for raw and manufactured materials.

19—Malcolm X's Birthday. Hold a discussion on the subject of "protest." Bring in early colonial personalities like Tom Paine.

20—Amelia Earhart began her solo flight across the Atlantic Ocean on this date in 1932. This was the first such flight by a woman. Discuss the opportunities for women today that did not exist in 1932.

21—Clara Barton founded the American Red Cross on this day in 1881. List some of the peacetime activities of the Red Cross.

31—Memorial Day. Commemorate this occasion by planting a tree or shrub in the school garden in honor of our fallen heroes.

Chapter 10

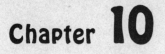

SUN	MON	TUES	WED	THU	FRI	SAT
		JUNE				

Each year the month of June seems to roll around more quickly. It seems like just a month ago that we were getting ready for Christmas and only a week ago that we returned from the Easter vacation. But the calendar tells us it is June and our memory tells us that this in many ways is the busiest time of the year. We've got to keep the pupils interested in school; if not we will be filling out accident reports all day long. One way to spark pupil interest is to . . .

Bring the outdoors in

June is a good time to prepare your children in the area of outdoor education or environmental or conservation studies. A group of sixth-graders in upstate New York participated in a three-day resident outdoor education program. The primary goal of the program was to develop in each child an ecological awareness and appreciation of the natural environment through using the out-of-doors as a learning and living laboratory.

Six major areas of instruction were provided: pond study, tree identification, astronomy, photography, nature walks, and a study of ecological succession. Independent student activities such as fossil study, bird identification, tracking, scavenger hunts, and "splash hikes" supplemented and reinforced subject matter instruction.

A highlight of the instructional program included the addition of a biologist and a forester provided through the state department of conservation. Further expert instruction was acquired through the local Audubon Society.

Teacher, pupil, and community reaction to the program was most favorable and plans are being developed to continue the program. Further information and details regarding this experience may be obtained by writing to Dale Hawkins, Sixth-Grade Teacher, Horace Mann School, 55 Ralston Avenue, Kenmore, New York 14217.

If you are interested in helping your teachers acquire more formal education in outdoor education, ecology, conservation, environmental education, or natural resources, there is a directory that identifies such colleges and universities, including the name and address to write to for further information. The directory costs $1.25 and is available from the Interstate Printers and Publishers, Inc., 19-27 North Jackson Street, Danville, Illinois 61832.

Getting information from parents

June is the month when you must finalize many plans for next year. In order to know just how many pupils you will have in your school you must get information from parents. For example, in some areas parents send their children to the public school for kindergarten but then opt for a parachial school in Grade One. Perhaps the non-public school does not offer kindergarten. You cannot assume that all the pupils presently in your kindergarten will move on to your first grade. Similarly, you need to know how many five- and six-year-olds are at home and plan to register for school.

The best way to get this information is to send home a notice with the children. Include a "tear off" at the bottom of your notice, as in the sample shown in Figure 10-1.

A similar form can go out to all the children asking if parents have any pre-school children at home whom they plan to register for either kindergarten or first grade. Such a form can also be used to get information on the utilization of school buses, hot lunches, a breakfast program, or any other data that you must have in advance.

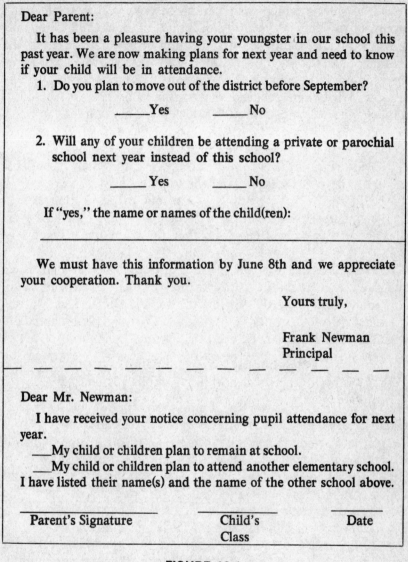

Dear Parent:

It has been a pleasure having your youngster in our school this past year. We are now making plans for next year and need to know if your child will be in attendance.

1. Do you plan to move out of the district before September?

_____Yes   _____No

2. Will any of your children be attending a private or parochial school next year instead of this school?

_____ Yes   _____ No

If "yes," the name or names of the child(ren):

_____

We must have this information by June 8th and we appreciate your cooperation. Thank you.

                      Yours truly,

                      Frank Newman
                      Principal

Dear Mr. Newman:

I have received your notice concerning pupil attendance for next year.

___My child or children plan to remain at school.

___My child or children plan to attend another elementary school. I have listed their name(s) and the name of the other school above.

Parent's Signature	Child's Class	Date

FIGURE 10-1

Examining the past year

June is the obvious time to evaluate what you have been doing this past year. Take time to determine how well your original plans turned out and to assess the quality of the tone and relationships within your school building.

One way in which to get frank responses is to invite small groups of students into your office for an informal chat. Be equally frank about the reality of implementing or rejecting some of the recommendations they make. Don't lead them on when you know the proposal is impossible. The students will probably recall some aspects of the school program that you have forgotten about. They will help you see things through their eyes. They will let you know which of your pet ideas are really working out and which are good on paper but not practicable.

These kinds of face-to-face contacts are absolutely essential if you are to have the pulse beat of the school. Think of the goodwill you're building when the pupils realize that you are asking them— the consumers—what they think are the highlights of the past year. Encourage them to tell you what they think are the low spots as well.

While meeting with these small groups, let your hair down and share with them the dreams you had for them nine months ago. How many were realized? Why did others fail? During this two-way examination of attitudes, objectives, and accomplishments, the students will see that you care about them and their needs.

Of course, you must reserve several hours to examine the year's peaks and pitfalls with the teaching staff. Did your schedules help improve instruction? Did you help each teacher find a growth area to which the person could point with pride? Was progress made in the variety of alternatives offered to the children?

School programs can be more relevant if all segments of the school population have a vocal and active part in devising them. Before the school year closes, be sure your examination of programs and personnel has left the impression with students and staff that the close of another successful school year brings with it your appreciation of the fact that so many have helped to make it so.

June is also the time when you have to contemplate what can be done to safeguard your building during the summer months. Reducing vandalism and pupil unrest is a year-round concern ... it just seems more important at this time of year. So, let's ...

Focus on reducing vandalism and pupil unrest

Larger and larger chunks of our budget are being spent on cleaning up after school vandals have set fires, spray-painted, broken windows, or upset files. The spring and summer months are particularly popular times for school vandals to strike or for a minor fight in the lunchroom to escalate into a near riot. Most of the reasons for this unrest lie outside the school. Some few schools, however, serve as a dehumanizing agent for many students. The unhappy students have actually "declared war" on their school. The impersonal school does not meet their needs, it makes them "look bad," and it is demeaning to their self-concept. They are turned off and put down by their school. Failure has become a self-fulfilling prophecy.

All school staff members, from the superintendent to the classroom teacher to the custodian, can take steps to reduce the possibility of violent acts by students and former students. This is not mere wishful thinking. It is actually being accomplished in many schools all over the country. We have excerpted some practical ideas for your adoption. For example:

In Franklin, Illinois, a basic reason for the lack of student vandalism is the Student Service Organization, a student-run discipline group. Sixty members, all student volunteers, supervise the lunchroom and study halls. Only the relatively few students who do not behave in the student-run study halls or lunchroom go to a special room supervised by a teacher. Rules are strict but fair and put in writing. Five of the rules enforced are:

- Don't play favorites. If a group of your friends are in one study hall, ask to be re-assigned.
- Don't bully others. Your goal is a quiet study-hall or lunchroom. Don't use your authority unless absolutely necessary.
- Don't violate the rules yourself. Example-setting is the first criterion for an effective leader.
- Don't directly confront a belligerent student. Supervision should not lead to conflicts or ill feelings. If this happens, contact your faculty supervisor or the principal for a solution.
- Remember that any student who makes a statement you might consider a threat is liable for suspension or expulsion. Report any unpleasant situations to the principal immediately.

In Oakland, New Jersey, seventh- and eighth-graders have become documentary film-makers, and school officials believe their efforts are responsible for reduced vandalism in that community. The youngsters take their movie cameras to the scene and record the effects of vandalism—the after-effects of a break-in, for example. They interview victims and the people who have to clean up and pay up after an incident. Then they splice together a film that is shown via closed circuit television to the school's 1,000 students twice during the year—before Halloween and in June before the summer vacation. Showings include commentaries by the student film team. One tape included pictures and interviews at four vandalized locations; a school, a church, an industrial park, and an abandoned house.

In one high school parking lot in California cars belonging to pupils and teachers were being vandalized. Tape decks, batteries, tires, and hubcaps were being stolen. Here's how larcenies were reduced from 35 a month to almost zero. An assembly was held for everyone who drove a car to school. Of the 300 students who attended, 293 volunteered to serve as parking lot patrols, in groups of six. "What we ask them to do is act as observers and reporters of incidents," says the school's principal. "We do not want them to take any overt action. When they see a car come on campus that does not belong there, the observer calls the security officer and lets him know about it." This has worked well in several school systems because, as one administrator says, the students have a vested interest in protecting their own property. The idea is to make them see school property too as something that belongs to them and their parents.

The New York City United Federation of Teachers has put together a collection of tips for the safety of teachers and students. Some of the highlights are:

- Teachers should admit no one to their classroom who cannot produce a pass from the office.
- Teachers should not be alone in the faculty lounge.
- Students should not be sent out of the classroom alone.
- Teachers should document the misbehavior of students who are dangerous to other youngsters as future evidence for suspension or referral.
- The surest way for teachers or students to prevent sexual attack is never to be alone.
- In halls and corridors, teachers should ask for identification from students they do not know; a simple "Hi" or "Hello" should be given first, to avoid a possible tense situation.

Your emphasis in preventing vandalism and pupil unrest should be preventative. Do everything you can to prevent problems and to defuse situations that could turn into a crisis. If you are interested in a detailed "crisis counseling" approach to your school guidance program, contact Gerald Mullins, Yerba Buena High School, 1855 Lucretia Avenue, San Jose, California 95122.

Now that you have secured your building and prevented future vandalism, let's look at . . .

Making the most of your plant resources

June is the busiest month of the year. All kinds of culminating activities are taking place. This is the time of year when one auditorium and one gymnasium do not seem to be enough. In an elementary school you may have found your gym schedule sufficed to keep the gym in use all year long without conflicts. Now that the weather is getting warmer, it seems that every teacher wants to take her class out to the school yard. Make up a simple form with days of the week and hours of the day. Place it over the time clock or sign-in book. Teachers will sign up for certain periods of use and you will have avoided future conflicts.

The music teacher in a junior high school is accustomed to working with the band in the auditorium. She has done so all year. Suddenly, in June, the senior advisor marches in with the senior class, ready for a graduation rehearsal. Again a simple "Auditorium Use" schedule would avoid this awkward situation.

The PTA executive board is looking for a place to hold a Tuesday morning meeting. You cheerfully offer the second-floor conference room. Shortly after they are ensconced, the school curriculum committee reports to their regular meeting place—you guessed it, the second-floor conference room. The moral of these stories is that you should have a master room-use sheet and use it!

Of course, any school program or activity can be spoiled if, on the day of the event, the teacher is absent. Encouraging good attendance among teachers is one of our biggest jobs. Current contracts guaranteeing a fixed number of sick days plus days for personal business represent a step forward for professional workers. It is a far cry from the days when teachers dragged themselves into school with a fever rather than lose a day's pay or incur the wrath of a supervisor.

This is in sharp contrast to some young teachers today who feel compelled to use up their sick leave each year—even though this practice leaves them with no absence reserve for when they may have an extended illness. Whatever the reasons, you will be interested in ...

Six rules for improving teacher attendance

1. Make your school a pleasant place in which to work. Encourage your staff to hold parties and socialize during lunch and after school. Hold a school picnic in the spring and/or a supper dance in the fall. If your teachers look forward to coming into the building each morning they will be less likely to call in sick.

2. Praise good attendance. Make the teachers who have excellent attendance feel appreciated. Write a note to any teacher who has perfect attendance at the end of the semester. Put up a "What do these people have in common?" chart over the time clock or sign-in book. Do this in January and list the names of those staff members who have maintained perfect attendance so far. It should be a sizable list. Do the same thing in June. Write a letter to each person listed in June, congratulating him or her.

3. Show concern for teachers who are absent. When they return, don't hesitate to ask them how they are feeling. If they were not really sick they will feel awkward answering you. Teachers who were out for health reasons will appreciate your concern. Because they know you care about them as individuals they will enjoy a greater sense of belonging and are less likely to feel like staying out of school.

4. Send cards to teachers who are absent for more than two days. Call teachers at home if they have been out for a week or more. Have your secretary enter on a calendar the birthdate of every staff member in your school. Have her help you remember to send birthday cards to all faculty members a day or two before their birthdays. This will give them quite a lift. By doing it in an organized way you will not leave anyone out and will not run the risk of offending anyone. We have seen disinterested, disenchanted teachers perk up when they got a birthday card from their administrator.

5. In June, post a tally of times absent and days absent for each teacher in your school. This will serve to help your payroll secretary correct any errors. But more important, it will, in a subtle way, show the staff who the frequent absentees are. Also, those teachers with very good attendance will get some silent recognition.

6. Make good attendance an attribute when you promote from within. If two or more teachers possess similar backgrounds, training, and experience, appoint the teacher with the best attendance. You can easily justify this by pointing out the importance of having this out-of-classroom post filled by somebody who has a proven track record of good attendance. Of course, you must have good attendance yourself if this argument is to hold water. There is nothing like setting a good example yourself.

Like so many things in the area of administration, you must not take everything personally. You are not the target every time a teacher stays home from school. You can encourage good attendance; you cannot guarantee it.

How you can reduce confusion on the last day of school

The last day of the school year is one that we anticipate and yet each year it seems to sneak up on us. Teachers with the best of intentions will go off to parts unknown leaving some details undone. One of the best ways to tie up loose ends can be gleaned from the letter that one high school principal sends to his teachers ten days before the end of school (see Figure 10-2).

TO: Staff of Hamilton High School
FROM: John McGinnis, Principal
SUBJECT: Closing School
DATE: June 14, 197___

Please check your copy of the *Teacher's Handbook,* issued to you in September, for detailed instructions concerning each of the following items. All of these items must be checked and turned in before you will receive your June paycheck.

FIGURE 10-2

___1. Make-up tests to be administered where needed or a statement signed by you that none of your students are eligible for summer make-up testing.

___2. Your grade book with all marks complete. This will be reviewed by your head of department.

___3. Your roll book with complete attendance summary (for homeroom teachers only).

___4. All keys (desk, room, closet). Place keys in an envelope with your name and room number on it. Any keys missing must be noted on the face of the envelope.

___5. Your Library Clearance Form indicating that all books have been returned.

On the last day of school, June 24, a table will be set up in the Faculty Cafeteria and staffed by our two assistant principals. Turn in the materials called for above. Each item will be checked by an assistant principal and initialed. Take this checked form to the General Office and one of the school secretaries will give you your check.

Please accept my best wishes for a happy and healthful summer vacation.

J. McG.

_____   _____
Teacher's Name   A.P.'s Signature

FIGURE 10-2 (continued)

Another good suggestion is for you to take a walk through the building with your custodian during the last week of school. Point out to individual teachers the need for them to remove certain items of decoration. Sometimes a teacher is so accustomed to seeing something in her or his room that he or she forgets it is there. This is especially important when you anticipate a room change for some teachers. The accumulated materials can be staggering. If you and the custodian give the teacher ample time to get rid of these items there will not be any hassle on the last day of school.

Make sure that the classroom keys are stored in a safe place over the summer. It certainly makes things harder for intruders if individual rooms are locked and the keys are not around. Be sure that you and the custodian know where the keys are stored so that there will be no chaos in September.

Example of a letter to parents of the graduates

Of all the form letters that principals send to parents, few are awaited with such interest as the letter to parents of the graduates. At last that day has arrived. This letter must give necessary detailed information as well as general congratulations. In no way is it to replace individually written letters to outstanding graduates. The sample shown in Figure 10-3 will trigger other ideas in your mind.

TO: Parents of our graduates
FROM: Miss Helen Lloyd Keyes
RE: Graduation Procedures
DATE: June 8, 197___

Thanks to your cooperation, encouragement, and effort your child will be graduated from Tyler Junior High School on Tuesday evening, June 18. We will hold our sixteenth graduation ceremony at 6:30 P.M. at the Strand Theater.

The theater is air-conditioned and sufficiently large to allow each graduate to invite four guests. Tickets will be distributed to pupils on the morning of June 17. Since there are no reserved seats, I suggest that you try to arrive before 6:00 P.M. so that you can park easily and have your choice of seating.

Because of the large number of graduates, we ask your cooperation in the following details:

1. Do not send flowers to the school or the theater. We do not have the staff or the room to handle them.
2. Do not come up to the stage to take pictures. I will be happy to remain after the ceremonies as long as necessary if you want to photograph your graduate officially receiving his or her diploma.
3. Please hold your applause until all the graduates receive their diplomas.
4. Remind your graduate to line up on the Maple Parkway side of the theater by 6:15 P.M.
5. Caps and gowns will be accepted in the gym office at any time on the day after graduation. Deposits will be returned at that time. The tassel may be kept as a souvenir.

This is a very happy occasion and I look forward to congratulating you in person at the ceremonies. Thank you again for your cooperation.

H.L.K.

FIGURE 10-3

END-OF-TERM CALENDAR
(issued the first week in June)

TEACHERS:

Please read through this calendar in advance so that you will be able to anticipate what has to be done.

- Observe all due dates; there can be no time extensions.
- Pupils are to receive worthwhile instruction through June 28.
- Check off each item on the calendar as it is completed.
- Be sure that all entries are neat, complete, accurate, and appropriate. Do not allow pupils to see record cards.
- If you have a trip planned on the day when material is to be collected, please see to it the day before.
- Do not give out any advance information as to class or teacher.
- Leave room decorations up until the 24th.

June

4— First clerical half-day. Children excused for P.M. session. Hot lunch served at 11:30 A.M. No refunds if absent.

5— Promotion sheets due in main office. Sixth-grade teachers send office cards, class cards, test cards, and health forms for transmittal to junior high.

7— Grade Six teachers send in names of pupils who are deserving of attendance, service, and conduct awards.

12— "New" class cards, etc., distributed to next year's teachers.

13— Senior Class Day

17— Second clerical half-day. Children excused for P.M. session.

You will receive a copy of:
Organization of the school.
Class composition sheet for new class.
You will complete:
Address cards indicating new grade and room.
Set of office cards including Emergency Contact Card.
You should have for each child:
Cumulative Record Card.
Test Record Card.
Health Forms.
Reading Card.

18— Finish report cards. Be sure to indicate "Promoted" or "Not Promoted." Also indicate the new room to which the child is to report in September. Make sure that the date of the first day of school (Sept. 9) is on every report card.

21— Audio-visual equipment and other material must be returned to the school aides in Room 114.

Kindergarten graduation in the auditorium at 10:00 A.M.

24— Make up new roll book. Send new roll book to the office for safekeeping.

Send promotion cards to the office by 1:00 P.M.

25— Graduation in auditorium. Bothers and sisters with notes from parents will be escorted by aides to the auditorium.

All class parties to be held in the afternoon.

26— Give out report cards.

Pupils dismissed at 12 Noon.

Complete old roll books.

Lock everything. Dispose of trash.

Fill out "Close of School" letter and turn in with keys.

HAVE A HAPPY AND HEALTHFUL VACATION!!!

SPEECH TO THE GRADUATES

Good morning and welcome to this the final assembly for our sixth-grade pupils.

This is a time for reflection and also for looking ahead.

As we reflect on the past year we see that this class possessed many gifted pupils. Your reading and math scores surpassed the national and district averages. This was a spirited class that displayed many attributes of initiative and independence. (Cite anecdotes.)

I hope that you will retain that spirit of independence when you enter junior high school (high school) (college) in the fall.

You have learned many things during your years at the_____School. In addition to the basic knowledge and skills you have learned how to think for yourself.

I hope that when you enter_____school in the fall you will exercise the ability to think independently. Don't fall into the trap of always following the crowd. Think for yourself and do what you think is right. Don't forget what your parents and teachers have taught you.

We have great faith in you and feel confident that you will live up to the expectations that your parents and teachers have for you.

As I look at the proud faces of your parents and your shining eager faces and recall your many achievements in school I am reminded of the old adage: "The apple doesn't fall far from the tree." I would like to say "Thank you" to the parents for sending us such nice apples.

From the Principal's Desk

Congratulations to our graduates! It is our hope that their experience at P.S. 12 has brought us together in a meaningful way so that graduates, their parents, and our faculty have been best served. It is our sincere wish that our warm and fruitful relationship be maintained.

May I take this opportunity to welcome the children who are entering our school in the fall. Parents can be helpful in making the adjustment of our younger pupils to school life smooth and rewarding. You are urged to cooperate with the school in following a few simple routines and requirements.

Every child presently attending kindergarten and the first grade will receive a slip of paper at the end of the year. This paper will have the child's name, new class, new room number, and the first date to report to school—September 8. All kindergarten and first-grade classes can be easily located on the first floor. Upper grade pupils will have this information on their report cards.

On the first day of school, parents should bring the children directly to their rooms. The room numbers are posted over the doors. If you have any difficulty, any member of the staff will help you. After a few days, all kindergarten and first-grade classes will line up in their appointed places on the first floor. It is best that you arrive with your child at about 8:30 A.M.

It has been a pleasure for me to work with the children and parents of P.S. 12 during the past year. I trust you will enjoy a most refreshing and healthy summer and return on September 8 for another gratifying school year.

Sincerely,

Dennis Gladstone
Principal

Chapter 11

SUN	MON	TUES	WED	THU	FRI	SAT
		SUMMER				

The close of school in June is not the end of the year for today's school administrator. From your own experience you have no doubt found that some of your most critical decisions are made during the summer: personnel changes, curriculum adoption, teacher training, budget preparation. Of course, the most obvious activity that takes place in many schools during the summer is summer school. That's why we would like to share with you some ideas for ...

Getting your summer school rolling

Much of the preparation for summer school takes place in the spring of the year. However, some of the pitfalls can be avoided during the summer months. In the past, some of the major problems encountered have been the selection of pupils, the registration process, the maintenance of accurate attendance records, and transportation.

Some major strengths have included the carefully selected faculties, small classes, and the many opportunities for small-group and individual instruction.

Advance planning and the formulation of guiding principles characterize the districts that have enjoyed the greatest success. A few of the points suggested by experienced summer school administrators are included here for your consideration:

1. Early planning, in March, should include administrators, teachers, parents, and students.
2. Policies should cover course offerings, and tie in with the regular school program, hours of instruction, and means of transportation.
3. The kinds of courses offered should satisfy the needs of the community. Will it be only make-up courses and remedial reading? Can advanced work be taken? Some districts find it desirable to provide cultural enrichment which cannot easily be offered during the regular school year.
4. The program and its purposes should be interpreted to the community through as many media as possible: radio, newspapers, flyers, etc.
5. Students should be referred to the summer school. Preference should be given to these students over the walk-ins.
6. Careful recruitment, assignment, and orientation of the staff are important. Preference must be given to specially licensed personnel, library, remedial math, guidance, as well as subject specialists.
7. Articulation should be smooth between the regular school and the summer school. Teacher's judgment of the pupil's ability as well as test scores and school grades should be available to the summer school staff. The work done in summer school and the pupil's achievement should reach the regular school promptly in September.
8. The administrator should be qualified and experienced. He or she should be deeply involved in all matters relating to the summer school, including the development of the budget.
9. Where room permits, non-public school children in the area should be invited to attend. Arrangements should be made to alert their parents to the program and to obtain pertinent school records for these pupils.
10. The summer school principal should supervise the program and staff just as he or she would during the school year. Faculty meetings, teacher-principal conferences, and group or grade-level meetings should be provided as needed and in accordance with good supervision.
11. The student's summer school progress should be reported to parents. This is usually done informally by a conference as well as by a written transcript at the end of the summer.
12. Definite plans should be made to evaluate the entire program. Parents, teachers, and pupils should have an opportunity to

react in writing to the way in which the summer school was run. Tentative plans should be made for next year.

A question that we are asked nowadays is "How can I get a summer school program?" Such schools are funded in a variety of ways. Federal and state money has been available as well as local school board financing. More and more schools are moving toward a self-sustaining summer school or summer day camp.

This procedure is a pay-as-you-go operation. In most cases the building, textbooks, and supplies are provided by the school district. The teachers' salaries are divided up by the number of pupils enrolled, and parents are assessed this charge in the form of tuition.

If you want to write a proposal for a grant or some other form of funding, you had better include this information in your request letter:

1. Will students residing in other districts be attending this summer school program?
2. Will there be a tuition charge?
3. Inclusive dates of program and total number of days.
4. Expected enrollment. Remedial or enrichment?
5. Will the library, gym, and lunchroom be available?
6. Will parental approval be needed for enrollment?
7. How will teachers be selected?
8. What transportation is available?
9. How will students be referred?
10. What follow-up procedures do you plan?

You will probably be bound to certain seniority and other fixed rules for the selection of teachers for summer school. Where possible, select enthusiastic teachers. Don't select teachers who "need an extra job" or who have "a lot of experience" only. The summer is long and hot. The pupils who do attend deserve the best, most stimulating teachers you can find. Don't settle for second best.

There will be lots of other students who don't want to go to summer school but would like to use the school yard or playground. And so here's an idea for ...

How to keep your summer playground maintained

We found this article in the Parent-Teacher newsletter of a city school and are including it for your adaptation:

In order to continue to provide a safe and clean creative play environment for our children it is necessary to maintain and oversee the park grounds and equipment on an ongoing basis and to supplement the maintenance work of the custodian. During the long days of summer the playground is used extensively by the entire community and receives far more wear and tear than during the school year.

Your help is earnestly needed one day (any time and day) a month during July and August to:
1) clean up and collect disposable items
2) rake the sand areas
3) maintain the existing level of sand around the base areas of the play equipment.

Please make it a habit to check the playground when you pass it, and to report any problems to the Chairpersons. Feel free to help maintain the play area any time you are there enjoying it.

Paul De Marco 868-7644
Mary Connelly 443-8054

Summer is a great time of year for children. Just being outdoors and not following a schedule helps them grow and develop. For handicapped children, a little more structure is needed. One of the great ideas we came across was ...

Focusing on arts for the handicapped

Why not use the summer months to help your handicapped pupils use art as a medium of growth? Administrators have found the following areas of improvement:

1. Creative drama alleviates failure associated with written words in deaf children.
2. Blind children score significantly higher than sighted children on tests of musical ability.
3. Music helps to improve the memories of mentally retarded children.

4. Notable gains have been seen in reading skills of emotionally disturbed learners after the introduction of an arts program.
5. Trainable mentally retarded children have made significant gains in classroom behavior, speech, and language skills through the motivation of the arts.
6. The use of music activities with exceptional children can improve their speech, help them to regain the use of limbs, improve their rhythmic sense and relax their muscles.

A recent "Very Special Arts Festival" illustrated, through live demonstrations, how music helps handicapped children to read and count ... how videotaping enables them to explore and document their world and sharpen their communications skills ... how movement and dance increase their awareness of mind and physical movement ... how making puppets leads to writing and acting original playlets ... how games and movement provide a challenge to independent thought and action. In the festivals, pupils instruct educators in the arts they have mastered.

If you are interested in using part of your summer to set up or visit an "Arts for the Handicapped Program," contact your state education department. At present only one million or 12 percent of all handicapped children out of an estimated eight million enrolled in the schools of the nation receive arts programs. Congress is trying to allocate dollars to the National Committee on Arts Education for Handicapped to establish and support models and demonstration centers to be located regionally throughout the United States.

Developing a student handbook

The summer is perhaps the only time when you can pause and reflect on developing a student handbook. There seem to be so many interruptions during the school year. Yet a handbook for students is a must for secondary school pupils. It helps welcome them to your school and tactfully gives them the rules you want them to follow. I'm sure you already have a handbook, but perhaps it needs revision. Let's look at some of the contents of some of the better ones we have seen:

TABLE OF CONTENTS

Try to make your handbook a joint effort with much input from pupils. The cover itself should appeal to young people. Encourage pupil-artists to design the cover. It may not look as staid as the Principal's Guidebook to School Law but it should have eye-appeal to adolescents. The reading level should be low enough for all the pupils to read it without assistance.

Another important publication that you can work on during the summer months is your parent-teacher newsletter. So, let's try...

Adding spark to your PTA publications

Parents of elementary school children are always looking for reassurance that the antics of their children fit into the "normal" range. Why not use some time this summer to prepare an article or two on what parents can expect of ten-year-olds, or seven-year-olds. You may want to focus on the curriculum offerings of a particular grade. To help get you started we are abstracting for you a newsletter article titled "A Year in Grade Three":

Our third-graders are encouraged to read a wide variety of materials independently for pleasure and information. At all times interpretive and word attack skills are emphasized. Third-graders are exposed to Basal Readers, SRA, individualized reading, programmed readers, and many other materials depending upon the needs and ability of the children. Book reports are required to encourage personal reading. On library visits, children begin to understand the nature of various reference books such as dictionaries and encyclopedias.

Third-grade mathematicians deal with sets, numeration, operations (addition, subtraction, multiplication, division), geometry, measurement, and problem-solving. Opportunities are provided for pupils to gain their own insights and make their own discoveries. Visits to the Math Lab provide first-hand experiences with many materials.

Our young scientists try to....
The third-grade social studies program....
In the area of Language Arts....
Art opportunities are provided for....

This kind of article gives your parents a bird's-eye view of what they can expect their child to be doing in school. It is best to get this in the paper early in the school year. It can easily be adapted for junior or senior high school as well. There you can have subject area specialists write about their departments' offerings.

Other ideas for inclusion in PTA publications that help add spark are:

Agenda items for PTA meetings
Family trips to nearby points of interest
Book reviews of child care publications
Career guidance information
College and scholarship information
Specialized high school offerings
Summer and part-time job opportunities
Other agency phone numbers and referral procedures
League of Women Voters non-partisan articles
Boy and Girl Scout information

Little League and sports schedules
Fund-raising advertisements and events
Door prize coupons to be brought to PTA meetings
Lists of pupil birthdays for the month

Ask your colleagues in other schools to mail you their PTA publications. You can get some good ideas from them that you can adapt to your particular situation. I'm sure they will also get some good ideas from you. Remember, there is really nothing new under the sun. It's all a matter of repackaging what has been found successful in the past.

Something that is "new" and yet is based on the thinking of master teachers and administrators of the past century is presently called "attitude training." It is extremely worthwhile, so let's see how you can become experts at . . .

Effecting change through behavior training

Jeff Coats has founded the Professional People Development Company of Gap, Pennsylvania. His company has helped hundreds of school administrators and managers relate better to the people they supervise. His attitudinal training workshops have been well attended for 14 years. During these summer months you can develop more success in effecting change in your staff if you use these ten specific beliefs of Jeff Coats:

1. That all motivation is self-motivation. No one can motivate another person except through force or tyranny.
2. That if the principal or superintendent does not know how to change his own attitudes he can never hope to help others change theirs.
3. That all teaching is self-teaching and all human development is self-development. We must help individuals understand the learning process and develop their own objective goal-setting capability.
4. That the authority figure (principal, superintendent) does everything reasonable to help others to be self-reliant with as little dependency as possible, except in emergencies.
5. That nearly all sickness and its resulting absenteeism is a culturally accepted way for coping with psychological stress.

6. That all negative emotions are habitually self-induced and can be eliminated through growth in self-awareness.
7. That all communicating is first with one's self before being projected out to others: therefore if a person does not know how he communicates with himself, how can he ever learn to communicate with others.
8. That maintaining human-relationship harmony by repressing negative feelings will only lead to self-isolation and degrees of self-destruction.
9. That conflict is a reality in any human relationship and must be faced honestly and consciously channeled for constructive results.
10. That any long-lasting learning in life is always difficult to achieve and when offered as being easy should create great skepticism in the listener.

Don't feel that just "thinking" during the summer is a waste of time. Constructive thinking about your relationships with staff members or others can be very productive and a good use of your summer months. Here are some ...

Tips for opening the climate of your school

By now you have, no doubt, read many articles on how school climate has an effect on learning. Here are some suggestions for projects that may stimulate your thinking about how you may wish to go about opening up the climate of your school:

1. Revise the school's grading and reporting system so that it is possible for everyone to feel that he or she is succeeding. Instead of a fixed "A" "B+" grade, have teachers write brief comments on how each pupil is doing in comparison to his or her performance at the beginning of the year.
2. Open the membership on the student council to anyone who has an idea for improving the school and is willing to work on it. Some kids would rather be caught dead than run for office on the student council. Yet they may have some compellingly good idea that they would like to work on—a band competition, for example.
3. Form a group to rewrite the school's philosophy statement and its book of rules and regulations so that what the school stands for is understood more clearly by everyone and so that these beliefs are translated into reasonable rules.

4. Take students and staff members on retreats or form in-school discussion groups designed to foster open communication, mutual respect, and understanding. Involve parents in this process.
5. De-emphasize "seniority" among staff members. Involve newer teachers in your inner circle of idea-makers.
6. Form a group of students to study some of the inconsistencies between your school's policy statements and the manner in which the school's programs operate. Cooperate with them in changing this.
7. Take a long look at "traditional practices" and see if they are meeting your current needs.
8. Involve your staff in making mundane decisions, like what color should we paint the lunchroom or shall we spend more money on duplicating paper or on textbooks.
9. Look for opportunities to involve parents in decisions that affect their pupils and are within their realm.
10. Talk, talk, talk whenever you can. Write fewer memos, letters, circulars, etc. Increase your face-to-face encounters with staff, pupils, and parents.

All of these things can be put into operation without your abdicating your position of responsibility and authority. At all times you must remain in charge. By opening up the climate of your school you will have a happier staff and student body to supervise.

What to do to bring about a calm opening day of school

There are several things you can do this summer to get your school year off to a smooth start in September.

One frequent cause for confusion in September is a schoolyard full of eager pupils who don't know where to line up or even what class they are in. When you ask their parents if the child is registered they say, "Yes, but I don't know what I did with the slip I got in June." You can avoid this gap in communication with a simple postcard. Have your secretary run a batch of postcards through your mimeo machine with this simple message:

Dear Parent:
We are happy to welcome your child back to school. Your child's NEW class is_____. Please remind him or her to line up with this class on Monday, September 9 at 8:45 A.M.

If you have any questions you can reach me at the school at 442-6123. I hope you have had a pleasant summer.

Louise Kennedy
Principal

_____
Pupil's Name

If you are afraid some postcards will misprint, you can run so₁ oak-tag the size of a postcard and then add a postage stamp.

Be sure to include the child's name since many parents will have more than one child in your school.

Have these cards ready in June or shortly thereafter. Then all you have to do during the summer is drop them in the mail three or four days before school opens. You will find that these reminders will not get lost. You can add a line: "Have your child bring this card to school on the first day." For newly registered children you may want to omit the word "back" in the first line.

Prepare class and room signs for pupils to hold up in the line-up areas. In pleasant weather you will probably want your pupils to line up outside. If the opening day is rainy you must provide a place in the gym or lunchroom. In any case, have the sign with the teacher's name and classroom in large letters.

Ask your school aides to come in a few days early to prepare kits of materials for each teacher. These should contain the essentials: chalk, lined paper, pencils, erasers, etc. With the kit of materials, usually delivered in a new wastepaper basket, should be a supply order request form in which individual teachers can ask for more specialized items of supply.

Similarly, have the school aides prepare sufficient quantities of each class' textbooks that they will be using. Teachers appreciate having these ready on the first day of school. It also avoids the confusion of having teachers or monitors scurrying through the halls asking for books and supplies.

The summer months are also a good time for you to check over your building and grounds to see that you do *not* have any violations of the local health or building code. Providing a safe and healthful environment in our schools is of great concern to all of us, and it is most important that we maintain constant vigilance in this area of administration. With this in mind, look over these . . .

Examples of health and fire department violations

1. Toxic solutions in unlocked cabinets.
2. Unauthorized electrical appliances in classrooms (coffee pots, hot plates).
3. Scatter rugs or objects placed on floor which present potential trip hazards.
4. Absence of a first aid kit in each classroom.
5. Crepe paper and other decorations that are not fireproof.
6. Irregular and infrequent fire drills.
7. Fire extinguisher or fire alarm box not in good repair.
8. Obstructions in corridors or near exits.
9. Unauthorized locking of exit doors while pupils are in the building.
10. Misuse of extension cords or overloading of outlets.

Check with your custodian to see if the exterminator came on stated intervals. If you have some classes eating lunch in their rooms, see if you can schedule them to use the lunchroom. It is impossible to keep roaches out of a classroom where 30 or more pupils eat their lunch daily. If all the pupils eat in the lunchroom, your custodial staff has just one area to clean up and keep free from infestation.

Now that the summer is waning and you are almost ready to re-open the school doors, make sure that you . . .

Make the most of the registration schedule

Spend a few minutes preparing a news release advising parents of new admissions to come to your school to enroll pupils who are new to the neighborhood or who are coming into your beginning grade. For example, here is a release that an elementary school principal sent out:

FOR IMMEDIATE RELEASE   (After August 21)

All public schools will be open for registration September 9, 10, and 11, according to the Hillsdale School Board.

Children who will be entering school for the first time and those who have moved after June 28 must register on these dates.

The students wishing to register must be accompanied by a parent or legal guardian and must have the following items for inspection by the registrar:

- Birth certificate or other proof of age. For admission to kindergarten, the child must have been born during 197__ , and for first grade, during 197__ .
- Report card or transcript from the former school if the child has moved to a different school district.
- A doctor's note approving the return of a child who has been absent from school for a medical reason.

If you have any question about these procedures, call Mr. Ray Hudson, Principal of P.S. 3, at 442-1020.

And now we have come full circle. We started this Almanac in September and proceeded through the year. This chapter contained ideas for your use of the summer months. Here we are, ready for another September and the opening of school.

We can't synthesize all the chapters into a single paragraph. But we have come across a short, simple bit of horse sense that we would like to leave with you as a kind of capstone to this book. When things get tough, and in our line of work they seem to get tougher every year, just remember this bit of philosophy mixed with common sense. It is called "Press On." We have seen it attributed to Calvin Coolidge. We have also seen it used by the McDonald hamburger people as a motto or watchword for their employees. It is included here for your use. We also use it to close our Almanac. There is no better way of saying "good-bye" that we have found for a book like this one. Here it is:

Press On

Nothing in the world can take the place of persistence. Talent will not; nothing is more common than unsuccessful men with talent. Genius will not; unrewarded genius is almost a proverb. Education will not; the world is full of educated derelicts. Persistence and determination alone are omnipotent. The slogan "Press on" has solved, and always will solve, the problems of the human race.

INDEX

A

After-school program, 56-58
Agency referrals, 55
American Indian Day, 40
Amerigo Vespucci, 154
Anthony, Susan B., 133
Arts program, 206-207
Ashura, 116
Attendance:
    pupil, 87-88, 100
    teacher, 112-113, 196-197
Attucks, Crispus, 154
Audio-visual equipment, 105, 124, 182-183
Audubon Society, 190
Awards Assembly, 171

B

Behavior modification, 74-75, 210-211
Better Breakfast Month, 41
Bilingual instruction, 103-104

Bill of Rights Week, 97-98
Black History Week, 133
Bomb scare, 125
Book fair, 144-146
Boston Tea Party, 101
Building security, 149
Bulletin boards, 61, 81
Buses, 43-44

C

Calendar, 200-201
Career Day, 141-144
Chicago Daily News, 115
Child abuse, 108-109
Chinese holidays, 117, 170
Citizenship Day, 40
Clean-up, 96-97, 132
Clubs, school, 89-93
Coats, Jeff, 210
Columbus Day, 59-60, 63
Community involvement, 107-108
Constitution Week, 40
Contract:
    non-renewal, 155-157

219